Cambridge Elements

Elements in Corpus Linguistics
edited by
Susan Hunston
University of Birmingham

AUTOMATIC IMAGE TAGGING FOR CORPUS LINGUISTICS

A Multimodal Study of News Representations of Islam

Paul Baker
Lancaster University and Zhejiang Gongshang University

Hanna Schmück
Lancaster University

Yufang Qian
Zhejiang Gongshang University

Shaftesbury Road, Cambridge CB2 8EA, United Kingdom

One Liberty Plaza, 20th Floor, New York, NY 10006, USA

477 Williamstown Road, Port Melbourne, VIC 3207, Australia

314–321, 3rd Floor, Plot 3, Splendor Forum, Jasola District Centre,
New Delhi – 110025, India

103 Penang Road, #05–06/07, Visioncrest Commercial, Singapore 238467

Cambridge University Press is part of Cambridge University Press & Assessment,
a department of the University of Cambridge.

We share the University's mission to contribute to society through the pursuit of
education, learning and research at the highest international levels of excellence.

www.cambridge.org
Information on this title: www.cambridge.org/9781009581240

DOI: 10.1017/9781009581233

First published 2025

A catalogue record for this publication is available from the British Library

ISBN 978-1-009-58124-0 Hardback
ISBN 978-1-009-58125-7 Paperback
ISSN 2632-8097 (online)
ISSN 2632-8089 (print)

Automatic Image Tagging for Corpus Linguistics

A Multimodal Study of News Representations of Islam

Elements in Corpus Linguistics

DOI: 10.1017/9781009581233
First published online: June 2025

Paul Baker
Lancaster University and Zhejiang Gongshang University

Hanna Schmück
Lancaster University

Yufang Qian
Zhejiang Gongshang University

Author for correspondence: Paul Baker, p.baker@lancaster.ac.uk

Abstract: This Element reports on the creation and analysis of a 1.5-million-word corpus consisting of a year's worth of UK national press news articles about Islam and Muslims, published between December 2022 and November 2023. The corpus also contains 8,546 image files which have been automatically tagged using Google's Vertex AI. Analysis was carried out on three levels: a) written text only, b) images only, c) interactions between written text and images. Using examples from the analyses, the authors demonstrate the affordances of these three approaches, providing a critical evaluation of Vertex AI's capabilities and the abilities of popular corpus software to work with visually tagged corpora. The Element acts as a practical guide for researchers who want to carry out this form of analysis. This title is also available as Open Access on Cambridge Core.

Keywords: corpus linguistics, multimodal, newspapers, Islam, image annotation

ISBNs: 9781009581240 (HB), 9781009581257 (PB), 9781009581233 (OC)
ISSNs: 2632-8097 (online), 2632-8089 (print)

Contents

1 Introduction

The exact origins of the aphorism 'a picture is worth a thousand words' are difficult to trace. It is sometimes attributed to advertising executive Frederick R. Barnard, who used a similar phrase, 'One Look Is Worth A Thousand Words', in the trade journal *Printers' Ink* in 1921. However, in 1918 an advert for a pictorial magazine called *San Antonio Light* contained the phrase 'One Picture is Worth A Thousand Words', and a similar phrase appears in a 1913 advert for the Piqua Auto Supply House, in Ohio. Even further back, an article in 1911 in the *Post-Standard* about a banquet held by the Syracuse Advertising Men's Club quotes the newspaper editor Arthur Brisbane as saying 'Use a picture. It's worth a thousand words.' We could go further back in time to hear the same sentiment expressed by Leonardo da Vinci, who said that a poet would be overcome by sleep and hunger before being able to describe with words what a painter could do in an instant. Even Confucius (c. 551–c. 479 BCE) has been credited with the phrase, having said 百闻不如一见 ('hearing something a hundred times isn't better than seeing it once').

No matter who came up with the idea or turned it into an aphorism, its meaning is clear – a message can be conveyed much more effectively in an image than in a verbal description. As Kress and van Leeuwen (2020: 16) put it, 'we see images of whatever kind as entirely within the realm of the realisations and institutions of ideology, as means – always – for the articulation of ideo-logical positions'. Images in news discourse are particularly powerful. Rafiee et al. (2021) write that such images 'call attention and raise awareness with an immediacy that text cannot easily achieve' as well as increasing the 'mass audience's emotional reaction toward social events' (1). The claim brings to mind an experiment by McClure et al. (2011), who found that image selection accompanying a relatively neutral news story had an impact on audience attitudes.

Images have tended to be disregarded in corpus linguistics research. Although a range of different frameworks exists for interpreting meaning in images (e.g. Kress and Van Leeuwen 1996, Peez 2006, Mey and Dietrich 2017), there is no agreed-upon standard, and the application of a framework would need to be carried out by the analyst, image by image; the equivalent of grammatically tagging a corpus by hand. Even if this was achieved, there are few tools which allow researchers to conduct an analysis of a large set of images or a combined set of images and written text.

However, this situation is changing due to advances in artificial intelligence (AI) which have enabled automatic taggers to work with images, assigning labels to them which describe their content. For example, Google Cloud's

Vertex AI uses machine learning to identify images from models pre-trained on huge datasets of images. The Open Images Dataset v7, from 2022, contains nine million annotated images which span 20,638 label classes.[1] In Baker and Collins (2023), a pilot study was carried out using Google Cloud Vision, a Vertex AI predecessor, with a small corpus (approximately 100,000 words) consisting of one month's worth of British national newspaper articles referring to obesity. Google Cloud Vision automatically tagged the 358 images in the articles with labels like Rectangle, Shoulder, Sitting and Event, resulting in around 29 tags per image on average. The tags were integrated into corpus files which contained the written text, and the pilot study analysed the resulting corpus with WordSmith Tools (Scott 2024), identifying both the keywords (i.e. words that are significantly more frequent in one set of texts when compared against another set) and the key image tags associated with each newspaper. A multimodal analysis was also carried out on the most frequent image tags. For example, the tag Event was found to co-occur in articles that also contained a lot of first-person pronouns. Qualitative analysis of these articles found that they tended to involve stories containing first-person narratives about people who had struggled with their weight and that such sympathetic representations were enhanced by photographs of them wearing smart clothes at public events.

Baker and Collins' (2023) study indicated that it was feasible to build and analyse a multimodal corpus, although its small size meant that it was difficult to obtain many meaningful results. Also, as the corpus texts were collected manually, the process used was not one which could be recommended for building larger corpora. It was also difficult to locate and view multiple images (e.g. all images tagged as Event) or images which co-occurred with particular text (e.g. all images occurring near text containing a first-person pronoun). Identifying such images also had to be carried out manually and was a time-consuming process. Furthermore, during the analysis, numerous tagging errors were logged, raising questions about whether the image tagger was actually worth using. Additionally, we should bear in mind that the set of tags for each image only gave a partial account of its meaning. The tagger was not perfect and tended to prioritise the tags it was most confident about. Even then, it was sometimes incorrect. Finally, some tags that might be useful for analysis (such as information about a person's sex) simply weren't part of the system. This meant the tagging system could not produce a set of tags which would tell us the overall message of each image. Instead, through analysis of repeated tags, the authors identified how particular aspects of an image can appear repeatedly in articles which have certain uses of language.

---

[1] https://storage.googleapis.com/openimages/web/index.html.

The aim of this Element is therefore to carry out a more comprehensive study, addressing the issues that were raised in the pilot study. Specifically, we wanted to (a) automate the process of building a multimodal news corpus; (b) identify the level of tagging accuracy of the images and find ways to improve accuracy if required; (c) develop a tool which would allow images to be surveyed if they appeared with certain tags or in newspapers that contained certain words; and (d) carry out a multimodal analysis on representations in a much larger news corpus in order to ascertain whether the visual and multimodal aspects of the analysis were able to bring new and useful insights to discourse analysis of newspapers as opposed to confirming a traditional analysis of the written text. Nikolajeva and Scott (2000) discuss the 'dynamics of word/image' interaction, noting how relationships between the two can be complementary (e.g. each giving similar information or where one mode amplifies or expands on the meaning of the other) or counterpointing (e.g. where words and images provide alternative information or contradict one another). While both kinds of relationship can be useful, it would be hoped that aspects of a visual analysis would provide more than a simple confirmation of the findings of an analysis of written text.

Rather than examining a larger corpus of news articles about obesity, it was decided to choose a different topic: Muslims and Islam. This is a topic which one of the authors had worked on previously, although only through examining written text corpora (e.g. Baker et al. 2013). In that study a 143-million-word corpus containing news articles from 12 newspapers about Muslims and Islam published between 1998 and 2009 was built and analysed. In one part of the analysis the authors compared the newspapers together by identifying the keywords most strongly associated with each one. It was decided to replicate that analysis on a similar corpus, using more recent articles that included images.

Our research questions are:

1. To what extent does analysis of image tags provide new insights above the linguistic analysis?
2. What are the distinctive representations of Islam and Muslims in nine UK national newspapers between December 2022 and November 2023?

As a byproduct of the analysis, we also considered the extent to which representations had changed or remained the same, compared to the Baker et al. 2013 study.

In Sections 2 and 3 we provide literature reviews, focussing first on research which has tried to carry out analysis of images or which has combined analysis of image and text together. The second literature review looks at news studies relating to the representation of Muslims and Islam, with a particular focus on corpus-related research. In Sections 4 and 5 we provide an account of how we created the corpus for this study and how we carried out the analysis. In Section 6 we outline the six stages of analysis that we performed on the corpus, which involved analysing distinctive words and images separately and together as well as comparing the findings of different parts of the analysis against one another. Finally, the Element has a concluding section which critically considers the value of building and analysing a multimodal corpus, along with directions for future research.

2 Integrating Images in Corpus Linguistics

A multimodal corpus can be broadly defined as one which contains more than one semiotic system (such as sound and moving images). Consideration of all of the different forms of multimodality is beyond the scope of this Element, and we are specifically concerned with those which contain written text and still images. Multimodal corpus analysis has required developments both in visual analysis and corpus linguistics, two fields which did not initially acknowledge one another very often. An early study, by Smith et al. (1998), described the creation of a corpus of children's writing, which contained a combination of text and drawings. In order to integrate the images into the corpus, the researchers coded each image with a single tag: <FIGURE>. Although no further information was provided about the images, there were hypertext links to online scans of the original texts so that the images could be viewed by analysts if required.

Prior to the emergence of online image taggers, images tended to be analysed by hand with user-defined categorisation schemes. Kress and van Leeuwen (1996) describe a detailed, multi-dimensional way of categorising images, considering phenomena like participants, processes, structures, colour, position of the viewer, modality and composition. It is unlikely that every aspect of the scheme could be feasibly implemented, especially on a large dataset, so more typically, analysts would need to decide which elements were most relevant to their research questions and the set of images they wished to analyse.

Some studies of news discourse have identified features that are not based on a generalisable scheme but on a small number of criteria that are relevant to a particular research focus. For example, Heuer et al. (2011) analysed photographs in articles relating to obesity from news websites, classifying them according to five criteria which were deemed to denote stigmatisation, such as images showing people eating unhealthily or images where heads and faces were not shown. Similarly, Collins (2020) created a simple classification scheme for images within Facebook posts, as well as annotating emoji. In his study, such labels could be counted as 'tokens' within keyword or collocation analyses.

Bednarek and Caple (2012) describe how images can construct the values by which some events or facts are judged as more newsworthy than others (Galtung and Ruge 1965). For example, they note how a news value like negativity can be shown by use of a low camera angle, to indicate the status of the participant in the image, or a high camera angle, which puts the viewer in a dominant position. Negativity can also be represented through pictures of people experiencing emotions like sadness or images of disasters and accidents. Subsequently, the same researchers used an integrated approach to identifying news values, called corpus-assisted multimodal analysis (Bednarek and Caple 2014). Corpus analysis techniques enabled the identification of keywords, frequent words and bigrams which pointed to different news values, while the images were analysed separately, then the two sets of analyses were considered together. In Bednarek and Caple (2017) a relational database was created using UAM Corpus Tool (O'Donnell 2008), where the codings of images and news headlines could be compared.

A similar approach was taken by Sibai and Jaworska (2024), who analysed representations of Saudi women in UK and Saudi news articles. For the visual analysis, the authors utilised the 'role allocation' part of van Leeuwen's (2008) framework, with images classed into four categories: agent (transactive), agent (beneficialised), patient (intransactive) and patient (passive). Chi-square tests were carried out on the category frequencies across newspaper types to identify whether there were significant differences in the representations. Then, separately, a corpus analysis was carried out on the text, which involved deriving and analysing word sketches (grammatically grouped sets of collocates) of terms relating to Saudi women, using the tool Sketch Engine and focussing on role allocation patterns. Subsequently, the two sets of results were compared through triangulation, with the authors finding that UK articles tended to represent Saudi women as driving cars visually more than textually, whereas Saudi articles tended to give equal space to both images and text for this kind of representation. Sibai and Jaworska (2024) argue that considering just one mode of analysis would have produced partial findings and limited interpretations.

While the above study considered the two modes separately, so could be seen as a 'mixed-methods' analysis as opposed to being multimodal, McGlashan (2016, 2021) carried out an analysis of a corpus of children's books which featured same-sex families, identifying keywords and key clusters and then linking them to the images they occurred with. For example, one key cluster – *love each other* – was found to relate to descriptions of such families, with members of the families described as loving each other. Examination of the pictures which occurred in the vicinity of this cluster revealed that family members were often depicted as hugging one another, which indicated that the meaning of *love each other* was implied to involve demonstration of physical affection, a facet which was not mentioned in the accompanying written text. McGlashan (2021) uses the term *collustration*, a portmanteau of *concordance* and *illustration*, to consider 'repeated co-occurrences between representations in linguistic and visual semiotic resources across numerous texts' (227). This kind of multimodal analysis was carried out by hand, so was restricted to a small number of linguistic items.

The process of tagging an image, either manually or automatically, is somewhat different to employing an encoding scheme to written text. Schemes like CLAWS (Garside 1996) and USAS (Wilson and Thomas 1997) apply part-of-speech or semantic tags, respectively, to every word in the corpus, and each word receives a single tag (although automatic taggers can sometimes suggest several possible tags in descending order of confidence of accuracy). For example, in the phrase 'Madonna hits album', part-of-speech taggers should assign a tag like 'plural common noun' to the word *hits*, although they may mistakenly assign a verb tag instead. In such cases, human annotators would notice the error if they encountered it. Conversely, an image tagging system would typically require multiple tags to be assigned to a single image, and it is not always easy for human raters to agree on their accuracy. For example, Gatt et al. (2018) report on a study which used crowdsourcing to annotate images of faces. Inter-coder agreement regarding the descriptions of the faces was variable, with coders having lower agreement on facial emotions or whether descriptions contained inferred elements. However, large datasets of images that have been tagged through crowdsourcing can be used to train automatic taggers, and it is in the current decade that we begin to see a new generation of visual analysis studies which have employed such taggers. An example is Christiansen et al. (2020), who used Google Cloud Vision to tag a large corpus of tweets. They labelled their analysis 'visual constituent analysis', and the study used the tags to create downsampled corpora on the basis of specified elements (e.g. tweets which mention Donald Trump vs. tweets which contain images of him). The written elements of the corpora were then analysed through a comparison of their semantic tags.

Todd et al. (2023) used Google Cloud Vision to tag a corpus of online advertisements, analysing it with their own tool (Multimodal Corpus Analysis Tool) to produce frequency counts of codes and to assess the likelihood of the co-occurrence of codes. Among their findings, they reported that there was a preference in the adverts for text to be positioned on the left, while pictures appeared on the right – a finding which went against general accepted theories of information value in multimodal texts. Additionally, most use of colour in the adverts tended to reflect accepted meanings (e.g. red means urgency), apart from blue, which signified familial love.

The pilot study (Baker and Collins 2023) described in Section 1 used WordSmith Tools to integrate analysis of Google Cloud Vision-assigned image tags and text, by analysing the keywords which appeared in articles that contained the most frequent tags in the corpus. As the corpus included image tags in the same position that the images in the articles appeared, it was also possible to carry out collocational analyses, for example, by identifying the words which frequently occurred in the vicinity of images that had been assigned a particular tag. The study in this Element aims to investigate this avenue further by building and analysing a multimodal corpus of news articles about Islam. Although we use the same automatic tagger as Baker and Collins (2023) – Google Cloud Vision – we should note that it has been integrated into Vertex AI, which is how it will be referred to from this point. However, before we describe our corpus of articles about Islam, it is pertinent to review relevant research which has examined news representations of this topic.

3 Representations of Islam and Muslims in the News

As far back as the 1990s, research on news relating to Islam in countries that do not have Muslim majorities has largely tended to report negative representation. Here we take representation to mean the ways that something is depicted through use of a range of techniques including evaluation, metaphor, narrative, connotation or argumentation strategies. Early studies tended to be small-scale and used a variety of methods, such as counting words deemed to be relevant, identifying topics and themes manually, or conducting qualitative analysis of argumentation patterns and discourses. For example, Awass (1996) examined American articles, finding that Islam was depicted as a threat to Western security as well as being associated with fundamentalism and terror. A 2001 study of Australian newspapers by Dunn (2001) reported that Muslims were constructed as 'fanatic, intolerant, fundamentalist, misogynist [and] alien 75% of the time, whereas positive constructions accounted for 25% of cases' (296). Poole (2002) combined focus group interviews with a quantitative analysis of a corpus of 1990s articles from four British newspapers, finding that British Muslims were frequently represented as criminal, extremist, irrational and antiquated, as a threat to liberal values and democracy, as involved in corruption and crime, and as influenced by Muslims outside the UK. Similarly, Richardson (2004) carried out a qualitative analysis of British broadsheets published in 1997, focussing on argumentative themes and concluding that processes of separation, differentiation and negativisation 'predominantly reframe Muslim cultural difference as cultural deviance, and increasingly, it seems, cultural threat' (232).

Such studies have tended to focus on news text as opposed to images, although an exception is Moore et al. (2008), who considered both aspects in their analysis of British articles published between 2000 and 2008. First, a content analysis (which identified themes and topics through close reading) of the written text focussed on types of stories, for example, finding an increase in stories which reported cultural and religious differences between Muslims and non-Muslims. The three most common discourses around British Muslims framed them as a terrorist threat and as dangerous/irrational and framed Islam as part of multiculturalism. Second, the visual analysis categorised people in images according to their sex, what they were represented as doing, what country was shown, whether people were alone or in groups and what the type of image was (photojournalism, police mug shot, cartoon, graphic, etc.). The authors found widespread use of police mug shots when depicting Muslim men, as well as images taken outside police stations and law courts. Muslim men were shown much more frequently than Muslim women and Muslims were often identified as Muslims rather than as individuals with distinct identities: for example, they were less likely to be shown in terms of their profession. A third part of the analysis involved qualitative case studies of a small number of articles, which identified cases where information had been exaggerated or distorted, such as the claim that parts of Britain were becoming Muslim-only 'no-go' areas. The analysis shows the value of considering different modes and methods in a single study.

More recently, large-scale corpus studies have been carried out on news representations of Islam, using software to identify patterns based on millions of words of data. For example, Baker et al. (2013) conducted a corpus analysis of 143 million words of British news articles about Islam and Muslims over a decade. Methods used included analyses of the collocational patterns of the words *Muslim* and *Islam*, and keyword comparisons of different newspapers and time periods. A key finding was that references to conflict were highly frequent throughout the corpus, with Muslims regularly represented as involved in violence, crime and terrorism, showing anger toward others, or being attacked or discriminated against. Terms relating to terrorism were actually higher than those relating to Islam, even though the Islam-related terms were the ones used to identify the articles to appear in the corpus. Articles tended to strongly focus on the news value of negativity, with few 'good news' stories or stories which reported on Islamic culture and traditions. Muslims were described as separate from other people, while there was evidence that conservative tabloid discourses around Muslims had influenced broadsheet reporting over time.

It is worth reporting on a couple of more recent studies, to obtain a better sense of the contemporary context that the current research occurs in. For example, Brookes and Curry (2024) created small corpora of news texts relating to Islamophobia in British broadsheets, taken from the years 2005, 2010, 2013 and 2021. They then identified keywords that were shared across each period, as well as those which had newly emerged, when compared to the previous period. They found that while there was initially scepticism about the extent of Islamophobia in the UK, and concerns about over-reporting, by 2010 there were moves towards equating Islamophobia with right-wing extremism and racism, with 2021 showing reference to institutional Islamophobia. While this study indicates a gradual improvement on one aspect of representation related to Islam, another diachronic study by Baker (2023a) presents a more mixed picture. This study considered use of words relating to terror and strength of belief (e.g, *extremist*, *devout* and *moderate*) over time in British articles about Islam. While such words tended to decrease over time when they collocated with *Muslim(s)* and *Islamic*, collocations of the extreme words with *Islam* and *Islamist* increased over time, indicating that newspapers had become more sensitive about associating extremism with the religious identity but were increasingly likely to connect the religion to extremism – a subtle but important distinction. These recent studies indicate a more mixed picture in terms of representation (at least for the UK), which raises a question relating to the extent to which there are differences between newspapers, as well as the role of images in news representations of Islam, both of which the present study seeks to address.

4 Data Collection

The corpus for this study consists of articles about Islam from the British national press, published between 1 December 2022 and 30 November 2023. Before describing how the corpus was collected, it is pertinent to consider relevant context and events, both internationally and in the UK, which help to frame the kinds of stories that were reported on around Muslims and Islam during the period under examination.

For example, 2023 saw the coronation of a new king, Charles III, after the death of his mother, Elizabeth II, in September 2023. The same year also saw the UK anticipating an election, with opinion polls putting left-of-centre opposition party, the Labour Party (under Sir Keir Starmer), in the lead, following increasing dissatisfaction with the ruling party, the Conservative Party, which had recently appointed its fifth leader, Rishi Sunak, in 12 years. In the election that took place in 2024, the *Express*, *Daily Mail* and *Telegraph* supported the Conservative Party while the *Mirror*, *Guardian*, *Independent* and *Sun* supported Labour. The *Daily Star* and *Times* did not back either party.

In terms of prominent stories relating to Islam, in Scotland, a Muslim, Humza Yousaf, served as first minister and leader of the Scottish National Party (SNP) from March 2023 to May 2024. At the time of his appointment he was the first Muslim leader of any Western nation. And on 7 October 2023, during the Jewish religious holiday Simchat Torah, the militant resistance group Hamas led an attack on an area controlled by Israel called the Gaza Envelope, using at least 3,000 rockets and paraglider incursions and killing 1,139 people. Of these, 364 were killed while attending a music festival, and 250 people (soldiers and civilians) were taken hostage. At least 44 countries labelled the attacks as terrorism, including the UK. Israel retaliated with attacks on the Palestinian territory called the Gaza Strip, bombing and killing members of Hamas and, as reported in the UN impact snapshot (UN-OCHA 2024), 15,207 civilians by the end of November 2023. The conflict led to protests around the world, including in the UK. Although these events occurred 10 months into our collection period, stories relating to them dominated the corpus, with the 10 most frequent lexical words across the entire corpus being *Muslim, Israel, police, Hamas, Gaza, year, Islamic, told, Israeli* and *years*.

When creating a news corpus it is common to identify a search term, consisting of words and phrases, so that articles containing those terms can be included. For this corpus, the search term was reasonably simple, consisting of just two words – *Islam* and *Muslim*. A more complex search term (involving 35 words and phrases) had been used in the Baker et al. (2013) study, although it was found that this resulted in a number of unwanted articles appearing in the corpus (e.g. the longer search term retrieved all articles containing the word *Sunni* and any related terms, and this resulted in unwanted articles which mentioned the village of Sunningdale appearing in the corpus). Even the term *Islam* resulted in unwanted articles, due to the fact that *Islam* is a surname, so when building the present corpus, concordance analyses of all instances of *Islam* were undertaken and 14 articles were removed.

In Baker et al. (2013), articles were collected from 12 British newspapers, and it was decided to replicate this model. However, one newspaper was no longer in print (the *Business*), whereas another (the *People*) was now published on the *Mirror* website. We also classed the *Observer* as a Sunday edition of the *Guardian*, as its stories appeared on the *Guardian's* website. Therefore, we collected articles from the websites of nine newspapers: the *Daily Mail*, the *Daily Star*, the *Express*, the *Guardian*, the *Independent*, the *Mirror*, the *Sun*, the *Telegraph* and the *Times*.

An advanced Google search was used to display all indexed pages on a given domain that contained the search terms. A model search for the *Telegraph* was as follows: *site:*https://www.telegraph.co.uk *"muslim" OR "islam"*. Additionally, the search selected the time span as being between 1 December 2022 and 30 November 2023. After identifying all URLs linking to articles containing the search terms from each of the nine newspaper websites using this approach, the URLs were scraped using custom Python scripts. As part of this process, the structure of each newspaper website was analysed and unwanted elements such as 'read more' or links to related stories, as well as overview pages and image galleries with no text, were removed. As part of the quality control on the scraped documents, several articles were identified that, despite being published on the dailymail.co.uk domain, contained Australian reporting. This is due to the fact that the *Daily Mail* hosts Australian articles on www.dailymail.co.uk/auhome rather than on a separate Australian domain. All such Australian articles were consequently removed. The last step of the data cleaning process identified articles mentioning Islam exclusively in the context of the name of martial artist Islam Makhachev and these were excluded also. When downloading the files, the full html was preserved and used as the basis for downloading all embedded images. Placeholders for the images at the relevant positions within the article were created, the downloaded images were named accordingly, and then the remaining html elements were removed. Alongside the articles, wherever possible the publication date as well as the names of the author(s) were recorded.

The resulting corpus comprised just over 1.5 million tokens and 1,890 articles. There were 8,546 images across these articles, which (after some tags had been removed, during the process described in Section 5) received 89,133 image tags in total. Compared to the earlier pilot study (Baker and Collins 2023), which utilised a corpus of 104,118 words and 358 images, this corpus is 15 times larger and contains 23 times as many images.

A detailed breakdown of the corpus is shown in Table 1. We have coded each newspaper with letters which indicate if they predominantly take a conservative (c) or liberal (l) political perspective, and whether they are broadsheets (b) or tabloid (t) format. We note higher numbers of articles in the *Telegraph* and *Times* (the two right-leaning broadsheets), along with relatively low numbers of images per article. However, the *Guardian* (a left-leaning broadsheet) has the fewest articles and fewest images per article. The *Daily Mail* has the most images per article and the most images in all (about a quarter of the total), while the *Sun* also has a high number of images. (Both are right-leaning tabloids.) The *Daily Mail* and *Times* have the longest articles (on average), while the shortest ones are from the *Express*, *Independent* and *Mirror*.

Figure 1 provides plots which show the number of words published on Muslims and Islam each day, for the nine newspapers. It can be seen, for example, that several newspapers (especially the *Daily Mail*, *Express*, *Independent*, *Sun*, *Telegraph* and *Times*) started showing more interest in

Table 1 Breakdown of the corpus by newspaper

	Total tokens	Total articles	Average length of article (words)	Total images	Total image tags	Average number of images per article
Daily Mail (c,t)	237,044	208	1139.63	2,350	23,155	11.29
Daily Star (c,t)	72,422	101	717.05	583	6,664	5.77
The Express (c,t)	119,123	197	604.68	843	6,694	4.27
The Guardian (l,b)	82,930	99	837.67	195	1,937	1.96
The Independent (l,b)	162,839	251	648.76	464	4,684	1.84
The Mirror (l,t)	153,412	221	694.17	922	10,151	4.17
The Sun (c,t)	171,919	241	713.35	1,493	17,518	6.19
The Telegraph (c,b)	228,087	283	805.96	633	6,996	2.23
The Times (c,b)	323,817	289	1120.47	1,063	11,334	3.67
Total	1,551,593	1,890	820.94	8,546	89,133	4.52

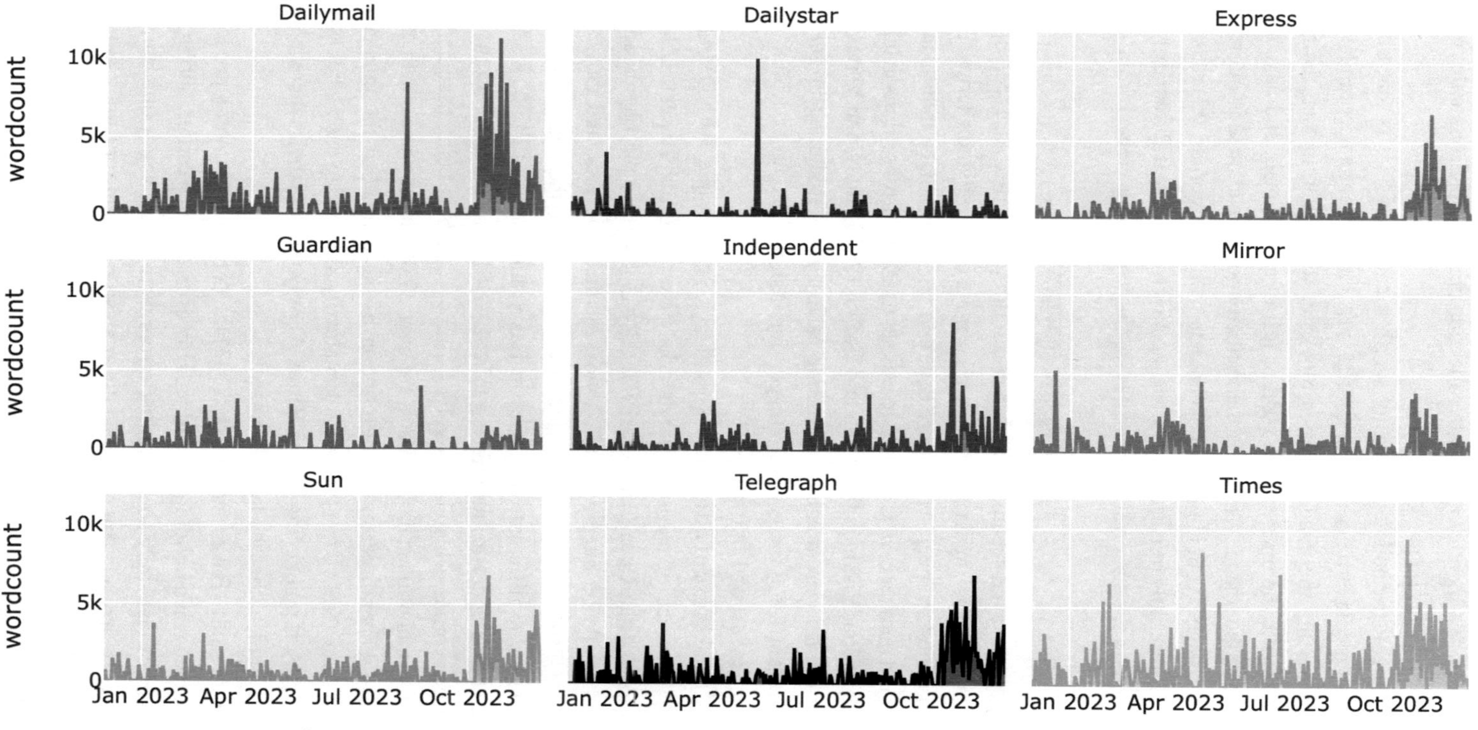

Figure 1 Overview of timelines showing the number of words in the corpus per day and per newspaper.

Islam in the last few months of our data collection period (which coincides with the conflict between Hamas and Israel).

A final general methodological point worth mentioning here is that transforming multimedia articles into a format suitable for corpus compilation necessitates placing the image between blocks of text when, in fact, the true layout might place the image to the right or left of a paragraph, and have text flowing around the image. While it is theoretically possible to include information about the page layout in the image metadata within the corpus, this runs the risk of misrepresenting true use cases since most websites have different display options based on the screen size of the device they are being viewed from.

5 Tagging the Images

Each image was saved separately and then run through Vertex AI, receiving a set of image tags. This, again, was achieved using a custom Python script. This script instantiates an ImageAnnotatorClient and tags each image individually. The maximum number of tags per image was set to 50 to mirror settings that had been used by CloudVision in the Baker and Collins (2023) study, and Vertex AI confidence ratings were obtained alongside each tag. After signing up for an account, the first 1,000 images were tagged for free, while it cost $1.50 to tag each subsequent set of 1,000 images.[2]

Vertex AI makes use of different classes of tags. For example, LANDMARK detects the presence of particular landmarks (like the Eiffel Tower), LOGO identifies logos (like Coca-Cola), SAFESEARCH identifies the likelihood of content that could be rated as adult, spoof, medical, violence and racy, and IMAGE PROPERTIES gives the dominant colours in the image. Having experimented with different categories in Baker and Collins (2023), we had decided that a category of tag referred to as LABEL was the most useful for analysing our corpus. This class involves a range of labels being assigned to each image (as mentioned earlier, there are over 20,000 label types), with each label being a generalised textual description of the content of the image. A confidence score (from 0 to 1) is also automatically assigned to each label, with the default cut-off point being 0.5, so Vertex AI only returns labels where it is at least 50% confident that the label is correct.

In the pilot study (Baker and Collins 2023) the default 50% confidence level was maintained when building the corpus. However, as noted earlier, during the analysis part of that study some tagging errors were noted, so for this study it was decided to carry out a more systematic analysis of tagging accuracy, aiming to improve it if too many errors were found.

---

[2] See https://cloud.google.com/vision/pricing/.

Table 2 Number of tags assigned to each confidence
level by Vertex AI

Confidence level	Number of tags
49–60	697
60–70	637
70–80	583
80–90	374
90–100	239

In order to determine the extent to which Vertex AI's label tagging was accurate, we took 100 images at random from the corpus and then two human raters independently assessed the accuracy of all of the tags assigned to each image. This resulted in the assessment of 2,530 tags, or 25.3 tags per image on average. Table 2 shows the distribution of confidence levels that Vertex AI assigned each tag. The average confidence score assigned to an image was 0.7.

Inter-rater consistency was reasonably good. The raters agreed that 1,508 tags had been correctly assigned, and also agreed that 508 tags were incorrect. There were 498 cases where they disagreed (so overall there was an average agreement of 79.6%). The 10 tags where there was most disagreement were: Electric_blue, Portrait, Advertising, Businessperson, Spokesperson, Flash_photography, Luggage_and_bags, Coat and Cap.[3] It was found that occasionally, the tagger assigned the same tag twice to a single image, and for the final version of the corpus, such duplicate tags were removed.

Based on the average error ratings it was found that Vertex AI was accurate 70% of the time. This figure was deemed to be not high enough to warrant using the image tags in the corpus, so experiments were carried out by raising the confidence threshold to a number higher than 0.5 in order to see how that would impact on overall accuracy. It was found that by raising the confidence level to 0.7, around half of the original tags would be removed, but overall accuracy would increase to 82%. This was an improvement on 70% accuracy but was still deemed to be too low.

It was then decided to identify the high-frequency tags and subject each one to a further analysis by looking at 15 images which contained such a tag. High-frequency tags which were assigned inaccurately most of the time could then be removed from all of the images. In order to determine what counted as a high-frequency tag, we plotted the number of tags against their frequencies. For example, there were six tags (AlloyWheel, Balloon, ContactSport, CosmeticDentistry, Dishware and Floristry) which occurred six times each in the corpus, whereas

---

[3] In order to aid our corpus analysis, we converted the format of tag labels to remove the underscore character. So in our corpus, the tag Electric_blue becomes ElectricBlue.

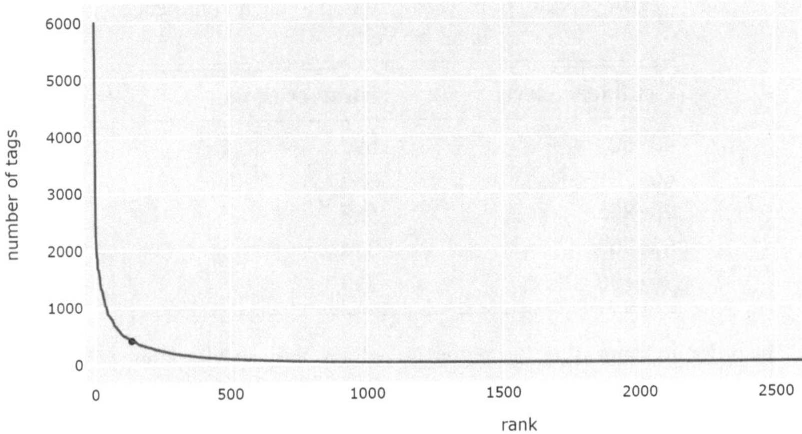

Figure 2 Number of occurrences of image tags.

there were two tags (Infrastructure and Leg) which occurred 99 times each. Figure 2 plots these sets of figures for all the tags in the corpus, with the x-axis showing the number of occurrences of a tag, and the y-axis showing the number of tags which have that occurrence. The curve in Figure 2 shows that the majority of the tags in the corpus only appeared a very small number of times, and conversely, there were a small number of very frequent tags (10 tags occurred at least 1,680 times each in the corpus). The point where the slope increases most strongly in the figure is at the tag that occurred 414 times (Bag) – marked as a dot in the figure. There were 135 tags that were more frequent than Bag, so we took all of these (plus Bag), and for each of these tags we selected 15 images at random that had been assigned that tag. This gave us 2,040 images to examine.

Again, two independent raters assessed the accuracy of each tag. Inter-rater consistency was found to be reasonably high, with an average percentage overlap of agreement of 0.79. The most accurately assigned high-frequency tags in the dataset were Building, Chin, Car, Human and Protest, whereas the least accurately assigned ones were Winter, Gesture, FashionDesign, AutomotiveDesign and Rebellion. This suggests that the tagger was somewhat better at identifying concrete phenomena (e.g. things that can be touched) as opposed to abstract or conceptual phenomena. From our sample, it was found that 96 of the 136 high-frequency tags were accurately assigned less than 70% of the time, so it was decided to remove all instances of them from the whole corpus. The accuracy of three of these tags (Beard, Moustache and Military) was slightly under 70%, but instead of removing them it was deemed that they were likely to be relevant to the analysis of the representation of Islam. These tags were included in the corpus, and in subsequent analyses we were careful to consider the possibility of tagging errors around them. The other 37 highly accurate tags were retained in the corpus, even in the cases where Vertex AI had assigned them a confidence level of lower than 70%. Having made these additional tweaks, we estimate that the overall average accuracy of tags had increased to around 90%, which was deemed to be acceptable to carry out an analysis.

So, to sum up, for the final version of the corpus, we first removed high-frequency tags that were less than 70% accurate. Then, tags with less than 0.7 confidence were removed, unless they were high-frequency tags which we had manually rated as more than 70% accurate. Overall, 20% of the tags in the corpus were below the 70% confidence level, but these were all high-frequency tags which had previously been deemed to have a high accuracy.

Figure 3 shows the number of images per day for each newspaper. It can be seen that the *Daily Mail* contributed more images than other newspapers, while the *Guardian*, *Independent* and *Telegraph* had fewer images. There are spikes for the *Daily Mail*, *Express*, *Sun* and *Times* in the latter months of the corpus (which coincide with the conflict between Hamas and Israel). Figure 4 shows the average number of image tags per image for each newspaper, with the *Daily Star* having images that were assigned more tags, generally, than other newspapers. As we will see later, this newspaper tended to have a high number of images containing people, so tags referring to body parts and clothing were frequent for this newspaper. Also, body parts and clothing tended to be easier for the tagger to accurately identify. In contrast, other newspapers might have been more likely to have had other kinds of tags, which were removed from the analysis because they were likely to be inaccurate.

Due to the multimodal nature of the corpus and the file requirements of state-of-the-art corpus software, it was necessary to store the image data in separate files containing the image tags alongside different versions of the traditional text-based components. CSV files containing the tags only were created, since it is recommended practice to run the image tagger only once and store the results in CSV or JSON files, for example, due to the environmental and financial cost of running the tagger.

An example of the structure of these CSV files is presented below, with each line containing an image tag, followed by its confidence level assigned by the tagger.

```
Face, 0.9832
Smile, 0.9771
Red, 0.8102
Beauty, 0.7497
LongHair, 0.7382
CompetitionEvent, 0.7234
HumanLeg, 0.6843
Chest, 0.6817
```

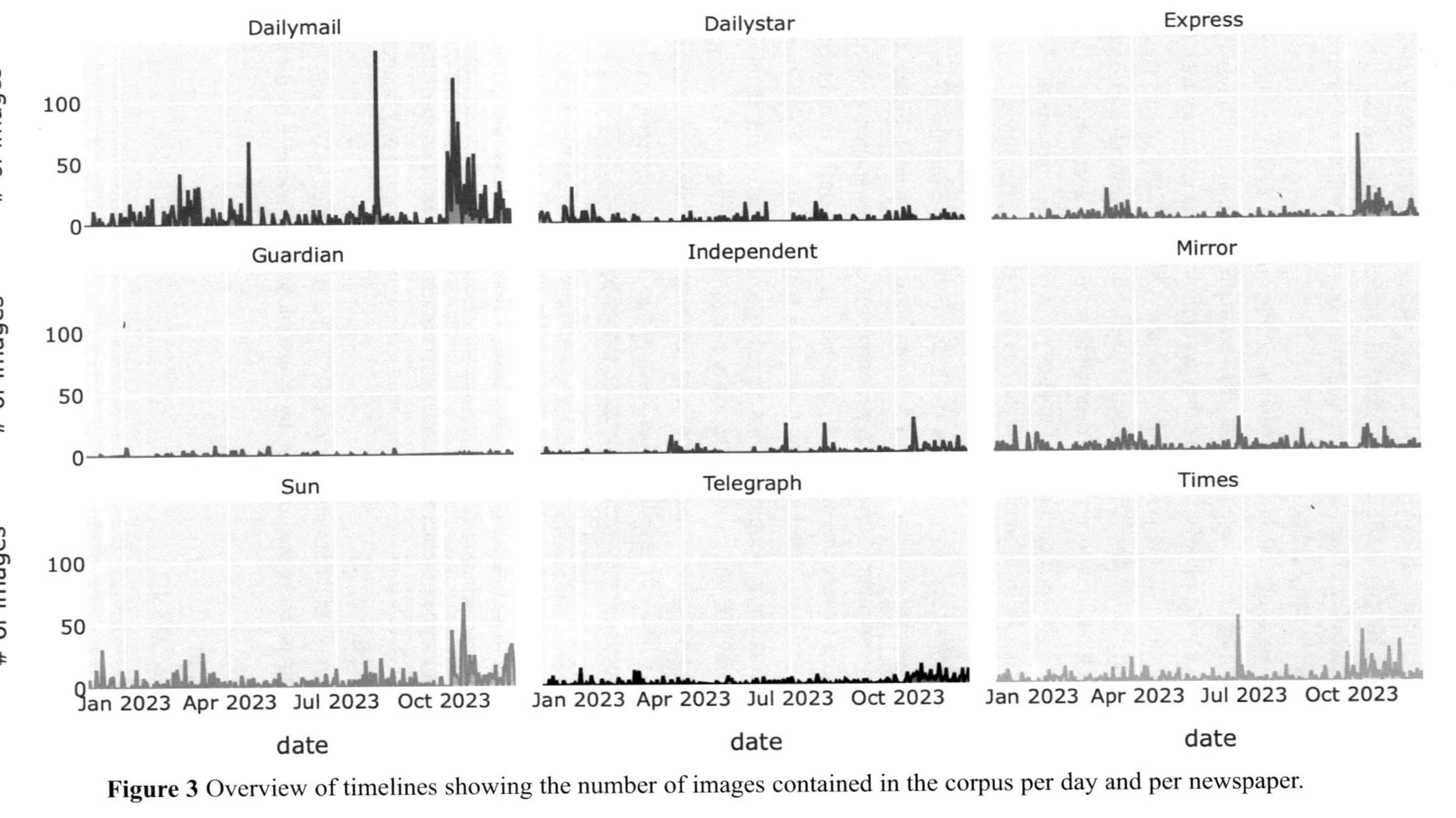

Figure 3 Overview of timelines showing the number of images contained in the corpus per day and per newspaper.

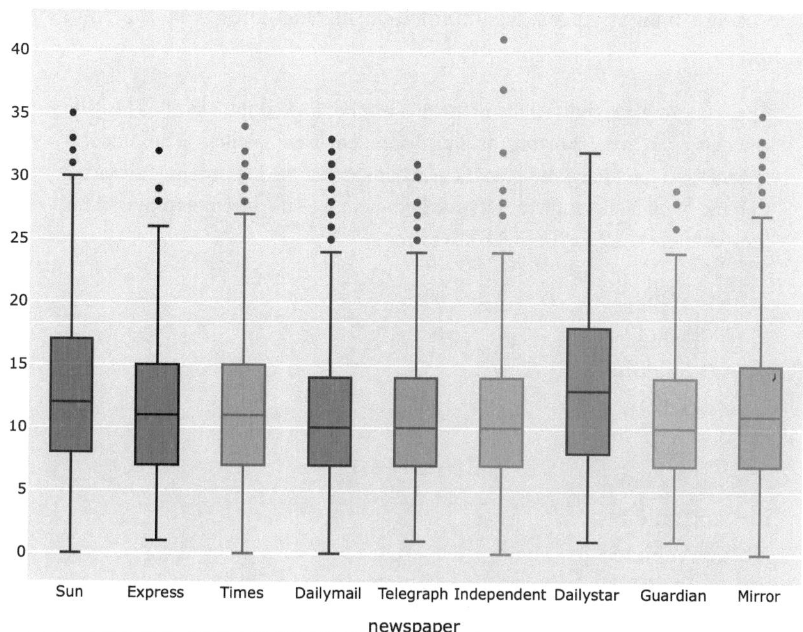

Figure 4 Boxplot showing the number of tags per image for each of the nine newspapers.

Sports, 0.6588
Grass, 0.6266

For the first textual version of the corpus, henceforth referred to as the 'development version', each newspaper website was accessed to identify the web layouts used and extract the textual elements relevant to the project. This entailed accessing the title, subtitles, captions where possible, and the body of the text, while excluding elements such as advertisements and links to further articles. Authorship and date information was also retained and stored separately for use in the XML version of the corpus, as discussed in the following paragraphs. In the development version, only the textual elements were retained, alongside placeholders pointing to the corresponding image files, as in the following excerpt:

.@@@Dailymail_2022–12–09_RachMusl_0_IMG_0@@@.
<title>Muslim nations 'proposed Islamophobia World Cup armband'</title>

After identifying appropriate thresholds for retaining or discarding tags on the basis of accuracy evaluations, a second version of the corpus, the WordSmith version, was created. Since WordSmith does not allow XML metadata to be imported, this version contains the text of each article with lists of image tags in

place of the images, using a simplified format, as shown in the following
example:

> Shocking footage showed the moment a teacher kicked the hands of Muslim
> students who were praying as she dismissed it as 'magic'. The students
> appeared to remain calm when the teacher entered the classroom and started
> to blow her whistle at them. Despite her attempt to disrupt their prayer time,
> they continued. RELATED ARTICLES.
>
> <xxxWater>
> <xxxLight>
> <xxxSnapshot>
> <xxxTree>
>
> .
>
> <xxxWater>
> <xxxBuilding>
> <xxxVehicle>
> <xxxTree>
> <xxxCity>
> <xxxUrbanDesign>
> <xxxAsphalt>
> <xxxRoad>
> <xxxGrass>
> <xxxStreet>
>
> .

In the excerpt above, after some initial text, there are two images, with their
respective tags delimited by full stops. This enabled us to identify collocates of
image tags within a single image in WordSmith, by treating each string of tags
as a 'sentence' and specifying that a collocate search should not run over
sentence boundaries. We assigned the letters xxx to the start of each tag to
make them more easily distinguishable from their equivalent word in the corpus
and to aid searches within WordSmith. (Note, however, that the xxx prefix has
been removed from the tags given in all subsequent examples.) The news article
files were saved as text only and were used with WordSmith when analysing just
the written aspects of the corpus, to carry out concordances, identify collocates
of words and create wordlists and keyword lists. This approach was taken to
ensure compatibility with the pilot study.

The third version of the corpus consisted of XML files containing the full
metadata (such as author, date and newspaper) and all text enclosed in <p> and
</p> tags (indicating paragraphs). The image tags and their confidence levels
are represented as follows in this version:

```
<img>< tag type="tag" weight="0.8814">Building</tag>
<tag type="tag" weight="0.7807">Gas</tag>
<tag type="tag" weight="0.7696">Heat</tag>
<tag type="tag" weight="0.6423">City</tag>
<tag type="tag" weight="0.617">Tree</tag>
<tag type="tag" weight="0.5664">Sky</tag>
<tag type="tag" weight="0.52">Asphalt</tag>
</img>
```

For this project, a simple application (called Image Tag Explorer) was created, which allowed the user to identify all of the images from a particular newspaper which occurred (or didn't occur) in articles that contained a particular set of words or had been tagged with a particular set of tags.

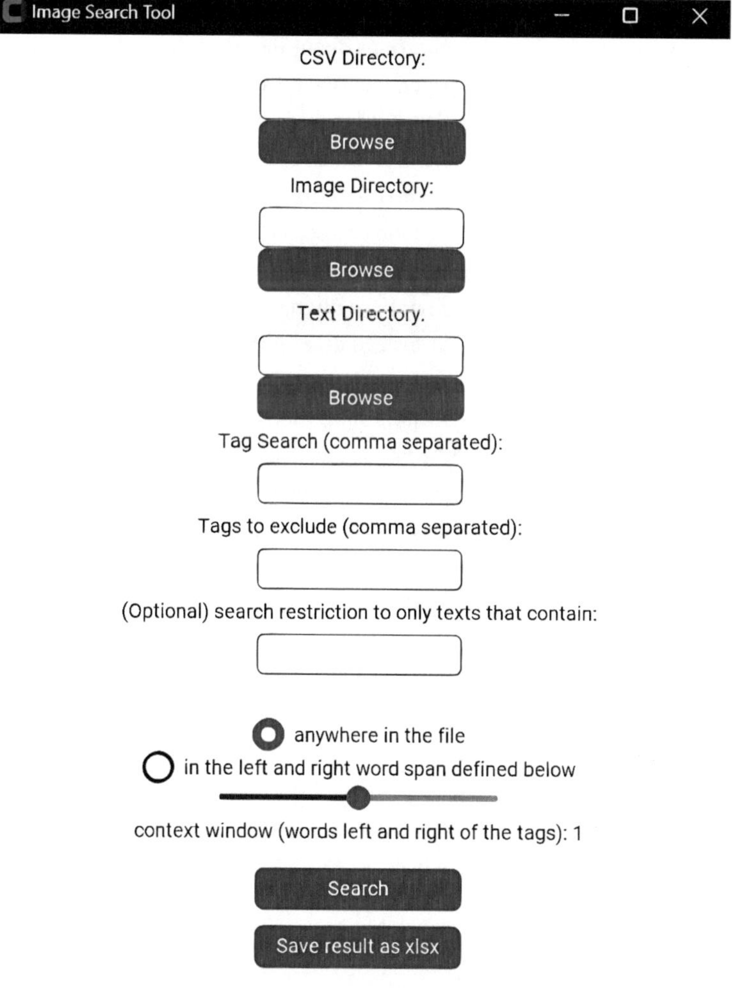

Figure 5 Image Tag Explorer.

Figure 5 shows the application's interface. The user specifies where the tags are stored (CSV directory), where the image files are stored (image directory), and where the XML version of the corpus is stored (text directory). Then, the user has the option to search for images with one or more tags, or images not containing one or more tags, as well as searching for textual elements that need to occur alongside the image in an article either anywhere within the file or within a certain span above and/or below the image.

After pressing the 'search' button, the tool shows the images from the corpus which match the filtering criteria, one at a time. The 'a' and 'd' keys (corresponding to backwards and forwards, respectively) can be used to cycle through the images. The rationale behind designing the Image Tag Explorer was that a manual inspection of AI-tagged materials is paramount in order to ensure their robustness.

6 Analysis

In order to answer the research questions about the most distinctive representations associated with each newspaper, we used the concept of keyness (Scott and Tribble 2006). Keywords are a concept invented by Mike Scott, the creator of WordSmith, and can be defined as words which appear in a corpus (or section of a corpus) statistically significantly more often than would be expected when compared against a second corpus or section of a corpus (Scott 1997: 236). A positive keyword occurs more often than expected, whereas a negative one occurs less often than expected. Keywords do not usually reveal the most frequent forms of language use in a (sub-)corpus but instead give an indication of words which are distinctive of it. A keyness analysis can help to reveal the preoccupations or biases within a set of texts which may be quite subtle and missed by human analysts. In order to obtain a list of keywords, a corpus tool is used to derive frequency lists of all of the words in the two corpora that are being compared. Then a separate statistical test is run on each word, comparing the relative frequencies of the word across the two corpora, as well as taking into account the total number of words in each one. Words are then listed in order of keyness strength, and users are required to impose their own cut-off point to determine what counts as a keyword. Most corpus software uses predefined cut-offs, although they can be altered to reduce or increase the number of keywords found.

There are several techniques that can be employed to calculate keyness, and generally a distinction is made between tests which prioritise the level of confidence that a frequency difference exists (even if it is not necessarily a large difference) and those which prioritise the extent of the difference. The former are sometimes referred to as hypothesis-testing measures, such as the log-likelihood test or the chi-square test, and they tend to result in lists of reasonably high-frequency words (as the higher the frequency of a word, the more 'evidence' the test has to go on and the more likely it is that the word will be identified as a keyword). The second type of test, referred to as an effect size measure, prioritises the scale of difference in frequency between a word across two corpora. These tests, like the log ratio test or %diff, may return relatively low-frequency words, where differences in relative frequencies are large. Both measures can be useful: log-likelihood tests can identify high-frequency grammatical phenomena, where even a small relative difference can be meaningful because we would expect all texts to contain grammatical lexis to some extent. On the other hand, %diff can identify extremely distinct, low-frequency items, which may otherwise go unnoticed by human researchers.

Although the term key*word* situates keyness within single words, it is possible to extend the concept to consider, for example, key lexical bundles, key morphemes or key sets of words. For the latter, it is possible to conduct keyness tests on automatically annotated corpora (e.g. corpora that have had tags assigned to words to indicate predetermined grammatical or semantic categories). For the purposes of this study, we carried out keyness tests on the words in the corpus, but we also carried out keyness tests on the tags assigned to the images in the corpus, in order to obtain lists of key image tags.

We used WordSmith 9 (Scott, 2024) to obtain and analyse keywords. In order to compare newspapers against one another, we derived a set of keywords for each newspaper, comparing it against a sub-corpus consisting of the other eight newspapers. We experimented with different settings in WordSmith in order to ensure that for most cases we could obtain at least 10 keywords for each newspaper, and that keywords would not be too infrequent, while relative frequency differences between the two corpora would not be too small. After our experiments we defined a keyword as a word which had a minimum frequency of 3, appeared in a minimum of 5% of texts and had a p-value (used with the log-likelihood test) of 0.1 or lower, as well as a Bayesian information criterion (BIC) value of at least 2.5, a minimum log ratio of 0.5 and a minimum dispersion of 0.1. The log-likelihood test and the size of the two corpora are used in the BIC formula. Gabrielatos (2018) suggests that a BIC of 0–2 indicates a word that is barely worth mentioning, whereas anything from 2 to 6 shows positive evidence of a keyword, and above 6 is strong evidence. When choosing keywords, they were ordered according to log-likelihood score. The same procedure was also carried out on frequency lists which consisted just of the frequencies of the image tags, to identify key image tags.

Once we had obtained keywords we analysed them by examining their collocates (both co-occurring words and image tags), and carried out concordance searches to view them in context. When a keyword occurred more than 100 times, we examined 100 occurrences taken at random to identify the range of uses, as well as typical and rare uses. We also used the Image Tag Explorer to find which images tended to co-occur with particular words, or which images contained various combinations of image tags.

Our analysis involved six stages:

1. Analysis of the written text through keywords;
2. Analysis of the images through key image tags;
3. Comparison of the results of stages 1 and 2 together;
4. Multimodal analysis – identifying words which co-occur with the top image tag in each newspaper;
5. Multimodal analysis – identifying image tags which co-occur with the top keyword in each newspaper;
6. Comparison and evaluation of the results of stages 1 to 5.

We provide details on each of these stages in Sections 6.1 to 6.6.

6.1 Stage 1: Analysis of Written Text Through Keywords

We began the analysis by obtaining the 10 strongest keywords (those with the highest log-likelihood scores) from each newspaper. In WordSmith's default settings, XML mark-up (i.e. anything which begins with < and ends with >) is ignored, so the frequency lists we created were derived only from the written text in the corpus, not the image tags.

As noted in the previous section, each keyword was examined through consideration of its collocates and concordance lines. (See Baker 2023b for details of how this kind of analysis is carried out.) The main questions we tried to bear in mind while conducting these analyses were: (1) what was the function of the keyword (typically) in that newspaper, or what kind of effect did it have in terms, for example, of semantic meaning, evaluation or discourse function? and (2) how did this keyword specifically contribute towards representation of Muslims or Islam? Different keywords called for different kinds of analytical foci. For instance, nouns and proper nouns relating to people or countries could be analysed in terms of social actor representation: what kinds of actions they were shown to be carrying out; what actions were done to them; whether they were evaluated positively or negatively; and, in terms of perspective, how much space was given to them to express their views. Adjective keywords were examined in order to ascertain what they were describing and the extent to which they were used in positive or negative evaluations, while verbs were also linked to social actors. Pronoun keywords were considered in terms of author–reader relationships and gender representation. We also tried to make links between keywords, particularly if they were used in similar ways or collocated with one another. Table 3 shows the top 10 positive and negative

Table 3 Top 10 positive and negative keywords for each newspaper (frequencies in brackets)

	Positive keywords	Negative keywords
Daily Mail	council (421), pictured (229), Friday (270), city (339), Gaza (641), Israeli (477), Israel's (104), students (194), her (1,300), Koran (105)	local (61), king (49), British (139), says (115), these (100), still (77), met (63), most (146), much (82), idea (10)
Daily Star	her (637), Knoll (62), king (140), Mia (60), fans (101), boxing (49), god (97), she (513), I (578), Croatia (44)	community (22), Friday (7), countries (6), hospital (10), groups (10), forces (8), last (50), clear (5), pro (9), or (108)
The Express	remembrance (39), Palestine (127), jihad (108), Sir (106), Keir (91), BBC (74), Mr (205), Met (104), pro (99), weekend (58)	women (45), council (28), him (103), released (22), prison (18), head (30), men (32), Tuesday (14), schools (18), south (20)
The Guardian	UK (227), prevent (112), promotion (44), Saunders (27), rightwing (29), coronation (68), review (68), royal (68), Charles (50), extremism (77)	show (15), off (23), me (50), social (20), just (53), ceasefire (11), ban (4), Arab (5), mosque (21), wearing (6)
The Independent	Muslim (833), Quran (174), Muslims (373), Mr (388), religious (253), Sweden (157), pilgrims (67), Hajj (74), said (1353), hate (197)	Israeli (73), her (447), Hamas (183), hospital (22), you (237), my (157), Iran (35), prevent (16), children (65), Syria (35)
The Mirror	Ramadan (258), Eid (188), fasting (126), you (550), your (215), it's (139),	Hamas (145), anti (33), Israel (187), political (15), its (155), minister (52), protest

            Corpus Linguistics

Table 3 (cont.)

	Positive keywords	Negative keywords
	calendar (55), life (245), fast (101), Isis (129)	(17), pro (19), Palestine (25), right (84)
The Sun	cops (86), rocket (119), hospital (224), Hamas (568), IDF (126), hostages (150), her (1,032), released (175), mum (110), blast (74)	that (1,197), Muslims (65), Muslim (268), religious (28), government (68), such (46), Jewish (32), council (31), law (36), protest (20)
The Telegraph	Mr (479), Iranian (188), Iran (259), IRGC (133), Iran's (90), Semitism (75), Islamic (530), its (603), anti (292), regime (111)	her (389), she (451), I (672), you (300), family (102), me (138), my (215), Muslim (421), show (50), life (116)
The Times	writes (66), Yousaf (150), Binyamin (34), politics (114), gay (107), church (139), Scottish (104), Scotland (101), political (223), conservative (108)	man (171), death (141), city (142), sun (17), letter (23), streets (43), claimed (86), holiday (20), terrorists (65), hijab (33)

keywords for each newspaper, ordered by keyness score. The positive keyness scores range from 576.55 to 42.40 while the negative keyness scores range from −420.37 to −7.51.

We began the analysis with a consideration of the *Daily Mail*'s top 10 keywords, three of which relate to the Israel–Hamas conflict: *Gaza*, *Israeli* and *Israel's*. To get a better idea regarding evaluation around the two sides of the conflict, we examined concordance lines of *Gaza*, identifying 100 cases of quotes or reported speech to obtain a sense of the extent that quotes were made either in support of or against either side. Of the quotes we examined, 78 made statements which showed support towards people in Gaza and 22 were against. Quotes against *Gaza* included those made by Benjamin Netanyahu. For example:

> It was barbaric terrorists in Gaza that attacked the hospital in Gaza, not the IDF. (*Daily Mail*, 17 October 2023)

On the other hand, positive quotes tended to focus on attacks on civilians, as the following statement from a group of Labour councillors indicates:

> The innocent civilians in Gaza have had nothing to do with this crisis and bear no responsibility for its outcome. (*Daily Mail*, 25 October 2023)

In order to compare this with the way Israel appeared in quotes in the *Daily Mail*, we decided to examine 100 concordance lines of *Israel* in which it was not a keyword, but was the equivalent term to *Gaza*, as opposed to *Israeli* and *Israel's* (which were keywords). For our concordance analysis of *Israel*, 49 quotes were supportive, while 51 were against. Quotes against Israel tended to focus on its bombardment of Gaza, for example:

> Israel continues to indiscriminately rain bullets and bombs on worshippers, murdering the old the young, attacking even funerals and graveyards. (*Daily Mail*, 8 June 2023)

Positive quotes focussed on the terror attack and kidnapping of Israelis by Hamas as well as criticisms of anti-Israel protests by Muslims (referred to as 'Islamists' in the second quote below):

> We have never before in Israel experienced such a traumatic event, which will take years, if not generations, to overcome. (*Daily Mail*, 12 October 2023)

> Islamists on the streets of London made 'completely reprehensible' calls for jihad against Israel. (*Daily Mail*, 22 October 2023)

The analysis suggests that the *Daily Mail* appeared more likely to quote people who were supportive of Gaza as opposed those who were supportive of Israel, at least in the period examined, which covers the first few weeks of the conflict.

The *Daily Mail* keywords *city* and *council* tend to occur together, referring to a number of city councils around the UK (including Birmingham, Leeds, Leicester, Manchester, Nottingham, Sheffield, Wolverhampton and Westminster). A closer examination of these instances indicates that they are from the same two articles, which both reproduce a letter signed by a large number of Muslim Labour councillors, asking the leader of the Labour Party, Keir Starmer, to call for a ceasefire in Gaza. These articles are unusual in that as well as printing the 461-word letter, they also list all of the signatories and their positions, amounting to a further 1,089 words. The publication of the letter thus represents the Labour Party leadership (which was not supported by the *Daily Mail*) as being in conflict with a large number of Muslim leaders in the UK. We also found during our examination of concordance lines of *Gaza* and *Israel* that there were a significant number of references to divisions in the Labour Party involving its stance on the conflict.

Friday stands out as an unusual *Daily Mail* keyword, as it is the only word in Table 3 which refers to a day of the week. Friday occupies a special place in Islam as it is when a community prayer service is held. The *Daily Mail* appears to mark cases where protests or other conflicts occur on Fridays:

> In the Iranian capital Tehran, hundreds of people marched after Friday prayers during which they burned a Swedish flag. (*Daily Mail*, 1 January 2023)

It is difficult to confidently interpret the significance of the *Daily Mail's* use of *Friday* in such stories, although one possibility is that the intention is to highlight a contrast between the scenes of conflict being described and the fact that they are marked as occurring on a holy day when Muslims carry out one of the most exalted Islamic rituals. The *Daily Mail* keyword *students* tends to relate to reports of conflicts at universities involving Muslim students, who are often characterised as taking unreasonable offence, for example:

> Muslim students force Minnesota college to close Iranian American artist's exhibition. (*Daily Mail*, 15 February 2023)

The *Daily Mail's* keywords therefore give a mixed picture, representing Islam through a lens of conflict and grievance, while quoting voices who show support for Muslims in Gaza.

Finally, we note the *Daily Mail* keyword *Koran*, which is sometimes used to refer to the Qur'an. The Centre for Media Monitoring recommends using Quran or Qur'an, noting that Koran is seen by Muslims as incorrect.[4] Across the corpus, there is considerable difference in how this word is spelled, as Table 4 indicates. The *Daily Mail* favours *Koran* over the other two forms more than any other

Table 4 Frequencies of *Koran*, *Quran* and *Qur'an* across the newspapers

	Koran	Quran	Qur'an
Daily Mail	105	12	3
Daily Star	3	0	0
The Express	7	35	2
The Guardian	0	0	1
The Independent	7	173	0
The Mirror	3	23	6
The Sun	8	6	2
The Telegraph	77	17	1
The Times	5	60	0

---

[4] https://cfmm.org.uk/term/quran/.

newspaper (although the *Telegraph* also shows a weaker preference for *Koran*). Most of the references to *Koran* in the *Daily Mail* relate to protests where it was burnt, kicked or stood on – actions that are seen as blasphemous in Islam. Numerous reports focus on reactions from Muslims at such demonstrations, for example:

> demonstrations have raged across the Islamic world after the nordic countries allowed the burning of the Koran under rules protecting free speech. (*Daily Mail*, 25 July 2023)

Such articles describe rather than denounce the attack on Islam and tend to instead focus on Muslims as angry about it.

The *Daily Star* has three keywords that are pronouns – *I*, *she* and *her* – indicating perhaps more focus on stories about women, as well as those involving a personal perspective. Closer examination of two proper noun keywords, *Knoll* and *Mia*, provides further information about the women who are most saliently represented in the newspaper. *Knoll* refers to the erotic photography model and former Miss Croatia, Ivana Knoll, who is the topic of 11 *Daily Star* articles about her presence at the 2022 World Cup, which was hosted in Qatar, a Muslim-majority country which has a dress code for women. Knoll is described as having sunbathed naked in Qatar and is quoted as saying:

> 'I'm not a Muslim and if we in Europe respect hijab and niqab, I think they need also to respect our way of life, our religion and in the end me wearing dresses, bikinis because I'm Catholic from Croatia who is here because of the World Cup.' (*Daily Star*, 2 December 2022)

Another *Daily Star* keyword, *Mia*, refers to Mia Khalifa, a British Pakistani who is an adult film star. Described as being brought up in a 'strict Muslim household' and no longer a practising Muslim, she is reported in the articles for having almost been banned from the social media platform Instagram for posting an almost-nude photograph of herself, and how she caused controversy by launching a new jewellery line called Sheytan, which translates to 'devil' in Arabic. Both sets of stories deal with young women who are seen as challenging gendered expectations in Islam through sexualised bodily displays. The articles aren't explicitly critical of Islam, but in terms of perspectivation they foreground the actions and views of Knoll and Khalifa, who are represented as being in conflict with Islam, through detailed descriptions of the two women, along with lengthy quotes from them.

In the *Express*, the keywords *pro* and *Palestine* tend to occur together, referring to pro-Palestine marches and demonstrations that occurred across cities in the UK. Coverage of the marches tends not to be positive, with marchers being referred to as 'a mob' or as 'leftie', along with reports that people at the marches chanted 'jihad' (also an *Express* keyword) and that they held placards showing

British and Israeli leaders with Hitler moustaches. There are also reports that one of the marches would take place on Remembrance Sunday, a day which commemorates members of the armed forces who died in World War I and all wars since, with the newspaper reporting concerns that the event would be disrupted by pro-Palestine demonstrations.

The *Express* refers to the public broadcaster the BBC and the London Metropolitan Police (both *BBC* and *Met* are keywords), quoting people who claim that the two institutions are biased towards Muslims and Palestine:

> Ex-BBC boss warns 'biased' broadcaster's Israel reporting is 'danger to British Jews'. (*Daily Express*, 22 October 2023)

> Rishi Sunak blasts Met Police for not acting on 'jihad' chants. (*Daily Express*, 23 October 2023)

Finally, the *Express* carries several articles about Labour Party leader, Sir Keir Starmer, which characterise him as coming into conflict with Muslims:

> Sir Keir was criticised for his refusal to call for a full ceasefire and his apparent support for blocking power and water supplies to Gaza. (*Daily Express*, 28 October 2023)

By representing the Labour Party and Muslims as being in conflict with one another, the *Express* can further create negative associations of two of its targets at the same time, much as the *Daily Mail* achieved by reporting on Labour's position on Gaza being different to that of Muslim councillors.

Three of the *Guardian*'s keywords tend to be linked to stories relating to the government's policy on extremism: *Prevent*, *rightwing* and *review*. Prevent is the government's counter-extremism programme, and the *Guardian* reports on a review of it which came out in 2023. The *Guardian* evaluates the review as 'controversial', 'ill-starred' and 'much-delayed' and prints quotes from people who are critical of it, for example:

> Britain's former top counter-terrorism officer has said parts of the government-backed review of Prevent appear to be driven by a rightwing ideology. (*The Guardian*, 8 February 2023)

Here, then, the *Guardian* represents Islam as unfairly singled out as a terrorist threat. Three other *Guardian* keywords, *Charles*, *coronation* and *royal*, refer to the coronation of King Charles III, which occurred on 6 May 2023. Although the articles in the *Guardian* question the relevance of the royal family and the expense it incurs to the UK, as well as mentioning anti-monarchy protests which coincided with the coronation, the newspaper also refers to the fact that this was the first coronation where representatives of different faiths were involved:

> One innovation is a greeting to the king to be delivered in unison by Jewish, Hindu, Sikh and Muslim representatives at the end of the service. (*The Guardian*, 4 May 2023)

On 30 April 2024, a Muslim MP, Shabana Mahmood, is reported as saying that she 'had already sworn allegiance to the king on the Qur'an and would be "joining in at the weekend as well"'. While the *Guardian* presents a somewhat anti-monarchist stance, it uses its reporting around the coronation to represent Muslims and members of other faiths as integrated and supportive of a key aspect of British society.

The *Independent*'s keywords appear to be more clearly focused on Islam than some of the other newspapers: *Muslim, Muslims, Quran, religious, pilgrims* and *Hajj*. These keywords occur in articles which provide readers with information about aspects of Islam. For example, *Hajj* and *pilgrimage* appear in an article entitled '"Hajj is not Mecca": Why prayers at Mount Arafat are the spiritual peak of Islamic pilgrimage'. Questions in these kinds of articles frame readers as interested in knowing about the Hajj, for example:

> What is the Hajj pilgrimage and what does it mean for Muslims? (*The Independent*, 25 June 2023)

Additionally, there is an implicature that the information provided in other articles is there because it is unlikely to be known by readers, for instance:

> All able-bodied adults of the Islamic faith are expected to complete Hajj at least once in their lifetimes. (*The Independent*, 29 June 2023)

Another *Independent* keyword, *hate*, occurs 47% of the time (94 times) as part of the phrase *hate crime(s)*, while 85 out of 100 cases of *hate* taken at random refer to incidents where Muslims have been targeted, with articles referring particularly to cases of Islamophobia as a result of the conflict between Israel and Hamas. One headline reads:

> Viral hate and misinformation amid Israel–Hamas crisis renew fears of real-world violence. (*The Independent*, 17 October 2023)

There are also references to incidents where demonstrators publicly burned copies of the *Quran* (an *Independent* keyword which, as seen earlier, is a preferred spelling by Muslim groups). Unlike the *Daily Mail*, which uses the dispreferred spelling, *Koran* (see Table 4), the *Independent* does not foreground anger of Muslims in these articles, instead referring 18 times to the burnings as *desecrations* (a term the *Daily Mail* uses just four times). The *Independent* therefore represents Muslims as engaged in religious observance, as well as being targeted for their religion.

Two of the *Mirror*'s keywords are forms of the second-person pronoun (*you, your*). A concordance-line analysis of 100 cases of these words taken at random found that seven cases involved a direct address to the reader (e.g. 'Do you have a story to share?') while 19 cases involved someone being quoted while addressing another person (e.g. 'I'm scared you are going to hurt me'). However, the majority of cases (74) involved *you* being used as a generic, described by Pearce (2001: 201) as a way of indicating commonality of experience (e.g. 'There are times in your life when you will be short of things and you have to accept what is happening'). We found that 52 of the 74 cases of generic *you* (72%) were used in articles which were written by Muslims and provided information about aspects of the religion. This also helps to explain the presence of other *Mirror* keywords *Ramadan*, *Eid* and *calendar*, which are similarly used in articles that provide explanations around the ninth month in the Islamic calendar, which involves fasting and is viewed as one of the five pillars of Islam. On the one hand, these articles provide an informative, non-judgemental and non-political perspective on Islam. Many of these articles appear to be written for non-Muslims, using the second-person pronoun to discursively exclude the possibility of a Muslim reader (something which was less common in the *Independent*'s articles which also provided information about Islam). For example, one article is entitled 'How to support your Muslim colleagues and friends during Ramadan', offering advice like 'give your colleagues time to pray', 'don't worry about eating secretly' and 'don't ask why someone isn't fasting'. Another notes,

> In a bid to support Muslim friends throughout Ramadan, you may be observing a fast yourself or celebrating Iftah with them, but another way you can show appreciation and care for Muslims throughout the month is by educating yourself on their culture. (*The Mirror*, 29 March 2023)

The 2021 national census identified 6.5% of the UK population as being Muslims, so these articles comprise an odd mixture of excluding Muslim readers while representing their culture positively.

Not all of the *Mirror* articles about Ramadan presuppose a non-Muslim reader. For example, an article entitled 'Ramadan: How to manage medications and health tests during the holy month' provides advice from a pharmacist called Ifti Khan, who is described as working at Well Pharmacy. Another article is entitled 'Best Ramadan chocolate advent calendars 2023 – from Amazon, Asda, and more'. The article goes on to list different kinds of calendars that are available and is written in the style of an advertorial. Therefore, these articles indicate how a positive stance towards Islam is interdiscursively linked to marketing discourse.

The *Sun*'s keywords tend to relate to war and terrorism, examples being *cops*, *rocket*, *IDF*, *hostages*, *released*, *Hamas* and *hospital*. *Cops* tends to be used to refer to suspected terror attacks carried out by Muslims. *Hamas* and *IDF* (Israel Defense Forces) relate to the Israel–Hamas conflict, as does *rocket*, which in 100 out of 100 random cases refers to rockets that were fired by those on the side of Hamas. One of the most commonly mentioned incidents involves a rocket that is described as having hit a hospital in Gaza (explaining why *hospital* is a keyword). However, this is described as being a 'failed rocket launch' by Islamic Jihad, and other *Sun* articles claim that Palestinians used the attack as propaganda, such as:

> Satellite reveals MINIMAL damage to hospital where Hamas claims Israel 'killed 500' ... after 'proof' it was a terror rocket. (*The Sun*, 18 October 2023)

The *Sun* discusses the Israeli hostages who are held by Hamas in Gaza, reporting on cases where they have been released, with particular focus on those who are vulnerable. For instance:

> At the moment they are the youngest hostages still remaining in Hamas captivity. (*The Sun*, 28 November 2023)

> Hostages have been seen in wheelchairs and with bandages on. (*The Sun*, 27 November 2023)

Finally, the keyword *mum* (as well as the pronoun *her*) tends to relate to dramatic stories, usually involving crime, about mothers who are Muslims. These stories can involve mothers as victims, as being related to terrorists or as a bad parent, as demonstrated in the following three examples:

> A neighbour has admitting killing a mum and her two children in a house fire. (*The Sun*, 21 April 2023)

> The school dropout was reported to the Prevent counter-terrorism programme by his mum, who had noticed a change in his behaviour. (*The Sun*, 2 June 2023)

> The mum, who converted to Islam as an adult, would allegedly report the children's 'bad' behaviour to her husband when he came home from work. (*The Sun*, 11 September 2023)

The *Sun*'s keywords generally paint a negative picture of Islam, implying that it is linked to war, terror and crime.

Three of the *Telegraph*'s keywords relate to Iran (*Iran*, *Iranian* and *Iran's*), while another keyword, *regime*, collocates 25 times with these words. Iran is represented very negatively in the *Telegraph*, being described with adjectives like 'aggressive', 'brutal', 'cancerous', 'decrepit', 'extremist', 'fanatical' and 'hostile'. In terms of carrying out actions, the *Telegraph* describes Iran as financing terrorism, suppressing women, carrying out executions and creating propaganda. There are eight references in the *Telegraph* to 'the Islamic Republic of Iran', and one article reports the closure of an 'Islamic centre in London that praised Iran terror general'. An opinion column accuses Iran of spreading conspiracy stories about Jewish people, asking:

> I might inquire of the Muslims who accept such stories: is Iran your idea of a worthy Islamic state? (*The Telegraph*, 16 October 2023)

Two other keywords, *anti* and *Semitism*, occur together in a fixed phrase, and tend to relate to situations where actions by Muslims have been characterised as anti-Semitic, as in:

> Husseini's task was to synthesise Quranic anti-Semitism with that preached by Hitler. (*The Telegraph*, 15 October 2023)

Thus, the *Telegraph* has a tendency to write about Islam in terms of international extremist and terrorist contexts, focusing on highly critical stories about Iran, which has one of the worst human rights records in the world (as opposed to, say, Muslim-majority countries like Indonesia, Bahrain and Oman, which have better human rights records).

Finally, the *Times* has three keywords which focus on the political situation in Scotland (*Scottish*, *Scotland* and *Yousaf*), relating to the leader of the Scottish Nationalist Party, Hamza Yousaf. He is described as a 'Muslim millennial, steeped in the politics of Independence' and some articles describe his election to the role as 'momentous'. An opinion column is more openly critical about Yousaf, noting that his election win

> shows our collective tolerance, forbearance and liberal-minded commitment to diversity: the fact that Yousaf is a Muslim or the fact that he is, by wide assent, formidably useless. (*The Times*, 2 April 2023)

The article goes on to criticise the 'liberal left which persists in seeing this country as "structurally racist" and everybody who is not white as suffering similar persecution by the white hegemony – a ludicrous mindset'. However, Yousaf is also described as having abstained during a vote about gay marriage in 2014, and the *Times* says he has been accused of hypocrisy. Linked to this, another *Times* keyword, *gay*, tends to involve stories about Islam's views on homosexuality, particularly cases which result in violence towards gay men. Typical stories are about Richard Rogers, a serial killer who targeted gay men and 'hated himself because he was a gay Muslim man', or Yousef Palani, a Muslim who murdered two men he had met through the dating app Grindr.

Other stories focus on countries with homophobic laws, which are described as linked to Sharia:

> Islamic countries which criminalise being gay are more populous, more likely to enforce their laws, and have tougher punishments such as the death penalty. (*The Times*, 15 December 2022)

Therefore, *Times* keywords indicate a representation of Islam as a religion which benefits from diversity initiatives in the UK, while at the same time being behind violence towards another minority group.

It is a little harder to explore the negative keywords in the table, as they involve under-use, so we need to consider possible interpretations relating to why some words occur less in some newspapers. For example, the *Mirror* and *Independent* (which both had some of the more positive representations of *Islam* in the corpus) tend to have fewer mentions of words relating to the conflict in Israel and Gaza. We also note how the *Times* had less use of some words relating to topics which have proved to be controversial in the past (see Baker et al. 2013), like *hijab* and *terrorism*. Finally, the *Telegraph* and the *Sun* are less likely to refer to the word *Muslim* than other newspapers, perhaps suggesting decreased focus on the religion at the level of those who practise it. (Both newspapers had quite negative representations of actions carried out in two Muslim-majority places – Iran and Gaza.)

6.2 Stage 2: Analysis of Key Image Tags

Table 5 shows the top 10 key image tags (both positive and negative keyness) associated with each newspaper, again comparing each newspaper against the others. Key image tag lists were derived by creating frequency lists which were only comprised of the image tags in the corpus. In WordSmith this was achieved by changing the tag settings in Advanced Settings to remove <*> where 'mark-up to ignore' was specified, then in the Part of the Text section, under Sections to Keep, < xxx and > were placed as the beginning and ends. This ensured that WordSmith disregarded all of the written text of the corpus, except for the image tags.

In essence, then, each image tag was treated as a 'word'. It should be noted that this process resulted in a much smaller corpus (consisting of 89,133 image tags), compared to the analysis of keywords, which took into account 1.5 million words. With that said, the same settings were still used successfully to derive key tags, although some of the tag frequencies are much smaller than those in the keywords table. While all the newspapers had at least 10 positive image tags, some had fewer than 10 negative tags.

To help us interpret the images, we used the tool which was developed for this project, called Image Tag Explorer (described in Sections 4). We used the tool to

Table 5 Key positive and negative image tags for each newspaper

Newspaper	Positive key tags	Negative key tags
Daily Mail	Crowd (621), City (629), PublicEvent (649), Street (486), Pedestrian (322), Rectangle (78), Protest (189), Pole (52), Screenshot (41), PublicSpace (97)	Trunk (41), Nose (100), HumanLeg (96), Knee (28), Hair (61), MilitaryCamouflage (35), Ear (48), Shoulder (48), Camouflage (22), Infantry (23)
Daily Star	Chest (131), Brassiere (52), Trunk (89), Undergarment (48), HumanLeg (124), Navel (42), LongHair (99), Lingerie (34), BlackHair (99), Waist (90)	City (36), Street (29), Building (19), Pedestrian (13), Crowd (51), Road (23), PublicEvent (77), Asphalt (13), Window (20), Vehicle (25)
The Express	Tie (116), Protest (62), News (12), Employment (70), Collar (77), Speech (65), SocialGroup (22), Chin (62), NaturalEnvironment (14), Gas (30)	BlackHair (19), HumanLeg (25), Cool (12), Shoulder (10), VisionCare (16), CompetitionEvent (29), Tire (30), Waist (21)
The Guardian	Organ (13), Ear (13), Brick (5), Speech (21), AerospaceManufacturer (4), Nose (20), Property (5), PublicSpeaking (17), Glasses (15), Employment (21)	HumanLeg, (4) Chest (4), CompetitionEvent (5), Car (5), LongHair (4), Asphalt (7)
The Independent	Room (80), PublicSpace (23), Employment (44), PublicSpeaking (34), Cheek (33), HumanSettlement (15), Protest (36), Wood (21), Trousers (13), Ear (20)	No negative key tags found
The Mirror	Cuisine (29), Dish (26), Cooking (22), Food (33),	Protest (14), PublicEvent (138), Crowd (133),

Table 5 (cont.)

Newspaper	Positive key tags	Negative key tags
	Recipe (24), Plate (22), NonCommissionedOfficer (38), Nose (93), Ingredient (14), Soldier (47)	PublicSpeaking (24), World (20), UrbanDesign (22), Beauty (19), VisionCare (27), Glasses (39), Wood (19)
The Sun	Gas (92), Shoulder (86), HumanLeg (149), Dress (40), Chest (142), Asphalt (163), Darkness (109), Trunk (85), Heat (44), FashionModel (41)	Protest (20), Crowd (199), PublicEvent (241), Tie (110), Jacket (26), Hat (191), Community (26), Cap (99), Employment (69), Speech (71)
The Telegraph	Protest (76), NaturalEnvironment (22), Handwriting (20), Building (121), SocialGroup (23), Speech (60), Temple (21), Community (36), Hood (15), Adaptation (21)	Eyelash (42), Grass (40), Cheek (20), BlackHair (25)
The Times	Tie (180), Speech (110), PublicSpeaking (85), PublicAddressSystem (42), Map (17), Landmark (26), Podium (20), SocialGroup (32), Shirt (23), Parallel (16)	Chest (19), HumanLeg (28), LongHair (27), Shoulder (18), Lip (32), Skin (22), Car (49), Hairstyle (22), AutomotiveTire (21), Beauty (20)

focus on a particular section of the corpus (e.g. just the *Mirror*). We could then specify one of the key image tags (e.g. Cuisine) and examine the corresponding images that had been tagged as Cuisine from that part of the corpus. In this way, it was possible to obtain a sense of the typical images that an image tag (or combination of tags) was assigned to. Additionally, we examined image tag collocates of other image tags, in order to obtain information about the ways that two image tags may often appear within the same image. For example, Table 6 shows the top 10 positive key image tags for the *Daily Mail*, indicating the frequencies of cases where two tags are assigned to the same image (with darker shades showing more frequent

Table 6 Co-occurring top key image tags in the *Daily Mail*

	City	PublicEvent	Street	Pedestrian	Rectangle	Protest	Pole	Screenshot	PublicSpace
Crowd	282	363	197	154	2	110	29	0	70
City	N/A	250	274	203	0	72	38	2	63
PublicEvent		N/A	280	202	0	188	43	0	28
Street			N/A	284	0	112	25	0	20
Pedestrian				N/A	0	77	28	0	16
Rectangle					N/A	0	0	5	0
Protest						N/A	7	0	3
Pole							N/A	0	7
Screenshot								N/A	0
PublicSpace									N/A

collocations). We refer to this as image tag collocation. It can be seen that there are a very high number of images which were labelled with at least two of the tags City, PublicEvent, Street, Pedestrian and Protest, while Pole and PublicSpace also co-occur in some of these images. Screenshot and Rectangle do not appear with the other key tags very much, although these two tags do co-occur in five images. Image tag collocation tables were created for the top 10 key image tags for all nine newspapers, which aided the analysis in terms of identifying particularly distinctive kinds of images associated with each newspaper.

When carrying out the analysis of the images, the contents of some of them were easy to identify, such as a picture of the then UK prime minister, Rishi Sunak, or an image of a demonstration with people holding signs reading 'Free Palestine'. For other images, we were sometimes unable to identify a person, location, building or event. In such cases we referred to the original news article or used an online reverse image search. For this stage of the analysis we wanted to focus only on the images, as opposed to the ways the images were written about, so we tried to identify only what was in the images, rather than attempting to interpret the ways they were discussed in the news articles. When analysing images from a single newspaper we tried to identify repeated features across numerous images as well as considering a range of other phenomena (see Kress and van Leeuwen 1996). For example, with images of people we considered: how many people were present; who they were; whether anyone was the main focus; whether people made eye contact with one another or looked into the camera or at something else; what gestures they were making; whether people were interacting; what actions they were engaged in or what was being done to them; what their facial expressions were like; and whether the images were flattering or showed them in a bad light. We tried to consider what kinds of emotions or associations the images evoked: for example, could the image be considered sexually arousing, upsetting, nostalgic or comforting? What kind of effects did composition or colour have in terms of how the image was interpreted? Were objects photographed from above or below and was symmetry or repetition used in the images to create particular effects? Analysing images is an interpretive and subjective procedure and we tried to avoid making claims that relied on implicature (e.g. that white clothing represented innocence or that the left part of an image represented 'the old' and the right part represented 'the new') unless there was supporting evidence for such interpretations.

We found that the *Daily Mail* was more likely to feature images of crowds in public spaces (indicated by images tagged as Crowd, along with City, PublicEvent, Street, Protest, Pedestrian or PublicSpace). Images assigned these tags often involved sports events (particularly football matches), demonstrations by groups of Muslims, Muslims at worship, particularly large numbers (in some cases, hundreds) of Muslim men in a prostrate position, called *sujud* (see Figure 6). These photographs were sometimes taken from an aerial position, making the worshippers indistinguishable, which explains the key image tag Rectangle, which was sometimes assigned to images where prayer mats were visible. In some images, Muslims are holding banners, copies of the Qur'an or simply raising their fists in the air. There is a sense of repetition within these images, with the people posed identically, so that visually there is a lack of differentiation between them. These images therefore echo one of the main findings of written news representations of Islam: collectivisation.

The key tag Pole also occurred in 52 *Daily Mail* images, including ones which featured Muslims holding banners or flags while engaged in demonstrations, protests or marches, and additionally appearing in street scenes, representing lamp-posts or street signs. An exception to these kinds of public group images involves around 50 which depict mourners (mainly middle-aged and older white women) in the funeral procession of the Irish singer–songwriter Sinead O'Connor, who died on 26 July 2023. Born into a catholic family, O'Connor tore up a photograph of the Pope on television in 1992 and converted to Islam in 2018.

Aside from the public gathering images, a second kind of image less frequently found in the *Daily Mail* (but still involving key tags) depicts screenshots from social media, which explains the tags Screenshot and Rectangle, over half

Figure 6 Muslims at prayer. Image from the *Daily Mail*, 10 April 2024.

of which relate to screenshots of tweets. These social media images tend to convey opinions relating to Islam, such as the conflict between Israel and Gaza or people's views on the eviction of a Muslim contestant on the reality TV show *Big Brother*. An analysis of the content of the tweets found that 29 of them had a broadly negative stance towards Islam, 15 had a positive stance and 13 didn't appear to reference Islam. The presence of images of tweets indicates how multimodal approaches can, incidentally, lead to an enriched context on the textual level since in some cases text is represented directly in a screenshot format. A monomodal approach would not have been able to account for text in this form.

The *Daily Star*'s key image tags all refer to body parts or underclothing, and examination of the images containing these tags indicates that the vast majority of them show pictures of young women posing in bikinis or underwear. Many of the women have long hair (hence the LongHair tag; see Figure 7). While Brassiere, Undergarment, Navel, Lingerie, Waist, LongHair and BlackHair almost exclusively relate to images of women, a minority of images assigned the tags Chest and HumanLeg involve pictures of sportsmen, particularly

Figure 7 Image of Ivana Knoll from the *Daily Star* (8 December 2022), tagged Smile, Brassiere, Waist, Undergarment, Trunk, Navel, Chest, Underpants, HumanLeg, Lingerie, Cheerleading, CheerleadingUniform, Bikini, Sports, CompetitionEvent, Uniform and PublicEvent.

boxers, wrestlers, footballers or rugby players. On the whole, though, the *Daily Star* appears to contain a higher number of sexualised images of women compared to the rest of the corpus.

The key *Express* tags Tie, Collar and News mostly appear in images of men in suits, particularly depicting political figures like Joe Biden, Vladimir Putin, Geert Wilders, Rishi Sunak, Nigel Farage, Emmanuel Macron, James Cleverly and Keir Starmer. There is quite a bit of overlap with the tags Employment and Speech, which also occur with pictures of political leaders, although these tags are additionally used with pictures of members of the British royal family, and also tend to include more images of British female politicians (e.g. Liz Truss and Suella Braverman). The tag Chin tends to be used even more generally, appearing in close-up images of the faces of a range of people – political leaders, celebrities, criminals, newsreaders and members of the public. SocialGroup tends to involve images of 2–10 people, usually involved in some sort of interaction.

A different kind of *Express* tag is Gas, which tends to relate to images showing large plumes of smoke, implying that a building or vehicle has been bombed. These tend to be images of urban destruction as a result of war. The tag Protest tends to show images of people demonstrating outdoors in large numbers. A survey of these images indicated that the highest number of protests relates to the Free Palestine movement, although there are also images of protests relating to trans rights, the pro-Israel movement and Brexit. Finally, a tag which links the previous two tags is NaturalEnvironment, which appears with images of both war and protest. Distinctive *Express* images therefore tend to involve political figures, protests or war.

The *Guardian* has a smaller number of images in its articles than the other newspapers (195, or 2.28% of the images in the corpus). Its key tags are less frequent than those for the other newspapers, with its two highest-frequency top 10 key tags occurring 21 times each, offering less evidence of distinctive patterns than with the other newspapers. Nonetheless, the *Guardian* sub-corpus contains a number of salient images which indicate a focus on close-ups of faces: Ear, Nose, Glasses and Organ (the latter of which also occurs with images of faces). Linked to these are the PublicSpeaking, Speech and Employment tags, which tend to involve images of people, often politicians, at podiums or using microphones, making speeches. Many of these speakers are well-known political figures. A second type of *Guardian* image involves the tags Brick and Property, which are associated with images of large public buildings. Possibly then, the *Guardian*'s key image tags indicate coverage relating to discussions about Muslims (by non-Muslims), which is related to politics and civic life.

Several of the *Independent*'s key tags are used in images involving large groups of Muslims, either at prayer or involved in protests (PublicSpace, HumanSettlement, Protest and Trousers – the last of which usually indicates the portrayal of a large number of men). Many of the images tagged Protest depict demonstrations by Muslims about the conflict between Israel and Hamas, with people holding Free Palestine banners or burning an Israeli flag. Another set of image tags relates to politics (Room, PublicSpeaking, Employment, Cheek and Ear). These tags typically show pictures of politicians, although they can also involve Muslims or images which look like mug shots of criminals.

Most of the *Mirror*'s top key image tags involve pictures of food (Cuisine, Dish, Cooking, Food, Recipe, Plate and Ingredient), showing either Muslims eating food (often in small groups which look like families) or close-up images of multiple plates of food such as rice, curry and samosas. Two other image tags, Soldier and NonCommissionedOfficer, show images of individuals in the military. Ten of these images are of a member of the British royal family, Prince Harry, who served in the military between 2005 and 2015, while the majority show pictures of other men, including the Iraqi general Abdul-Wahab al-Saadi and Scottish Muslim paramedic Araf Saddiq.

For the *Sun* images, three key tags are used for depictions of explosions: Gas, Darkness and Heat. These images often show buildings or vehicles which are on fire, giving off smoke and flames. A second type of image was assigned the tags Shoulder, HumanLeg, Dress, Chest, Trunk and FashionModel. This type of image tends to show full-body images of people, usually young women or sports players, often posed in provocative positions and/or wearing swimwear or showing cleavage. The two image types most significantly associated with the *Sun* therefore involve attacks on objects (relating to armed conflict) and sexualised photographs of women (similar to the *Daily Star*).

Several of the *Telegraph*'s key image tags relate to demonstrations (Protest, Community, SocialGroup and NaturalEnvironment), whereas Handwriting typically involves images of banners and placards which have writing on them, sometimes in Arabic. Placards in the Protest images show very negative representations of Israel and various politicians. For example, there are pictures of Rishi Sunak entitled 'Sunak, you are a murderer' or 'Crime Minister'. One poster shows a snake with a Star of David encircling the planet. Another shows Joe Biden wearing devil horns and fangs, labelled 'The puppet master, the mastermind of all evils'. A further poster states 'Kill Geert'. The image tag Hood also appears with images where protesters and soldiers are wearing head coverings. The tag Speech tends not to occur with images of demonstrations, but instead involves pictures of politicians around the world. Adaptation, Building and Temple involve images of buildings which sometimes feature Islamic architecture, including arches and domes.

Finally, for the *Times* there are three types of distinctive images. First, the tags Tie, Shirt, Speech, PublicSpeaking, PublicAddressSystem and Podium are assigned to pictures of politicians or other public figures making public speeches, including the leader of the SNP, Humza Yousaf, the member of the Scottish Labour Party Anas Sarwar, anti-Islam populists Geert Wilders and Marine Le Pen, the US president Joe Biden, and Hamas member Zaher Birawi. Second, the tags Map and Parallel are used for images of maps, which usually depict information such as terror attacks, zones of armed conflict or routes for protests. Finally, the tag Landmark shows a range of large buildings, including the Blue Mosque, in Turkey, the Giza pyramids and the City of the Dead (a cemetery complex), in Egypt, and Masjid al-Haram (Grand Mosque), in the holy city of Mecca, Saudi Arabia.

The analysis of key image tags gave us an indication of some of the kinds of contexts or topics in which Islam and Muslims are written about. It is worth noting that two newspapers (the *Daily Star* and the *Sun*) used eroticised pictures of women in these articles, while others (the *Independent, Express, Sun* and *Telegraph*) showed images of war and protest. It is also interesting to see how some newspapers (the *Express, Guardian, Independent* and *Times*) focused more on politicians, while others showed more cultural aspects of Islam to do with food (the *Mirror*) or architecture (the *Times*). One of the most interesting findings to emerge from the analysis of key image tags was the *Daily Mail*'s use of images showing Muslims engaging in collective worship behaviours. Additionally, it was interesting to see how the *Daily Mail* used screenshots of social media posts in its articles, whereas the *Times* made significant use of maps. Looking at the images without text, we get a sense of some of the contexts that Muslims and Islam are represented in (e.g. war, protest, architecture, religious observance, politics and family life), but beyond this it is difficult to fully grasp a more detailed picture at this stage.

6.3 Stage 3: Comparison of the Keyword and Key Image Tag Analyses

Having completed stages 1 and 2, we were able to carry out a mixed-methods analysis by comparing the keywords and key image tags from each newspaper together. This indicated how, at times, a newspaper's keywords and key image tags could relate to the same kind of topic. For example, the *Mirror* had a relatively high number of stories about Ramadan, and it also contained more images of food compared to other newspapers. On the other hand, some of the key image tags revealed other aspects of articles which were not revealed by the keywords. The *Daily Mail*, for instance, made relatively more use of social media posts as images in its articles, whereas the *Times* contained more pictures of maps. Neither of these kinds of images appears to be connected to the top keywords, and the images indicate different journalistic practices that might have been otherwise missed. In this case, social media posts are used to indicate people's stances on a news topic and also to show how a news topic is currently seen as important, while maps help readers understand stories about places they may not be familiar with. Also, the images of large numbers of Muslims at prayer in the *Daily Mail* were not indicated through the keyword analysis, nor were we expecting to see a relatively high number of images of people in the military in the *Mirror*, based on its keywords. So even when considering the keywords and key image tags separately, it is clear that there is value in looking at the key image tags, as they help to bring to light aspects of the articles which are foregrounded in the visual parts but which were not identified in the analysis of the written text. Similarly, there are aspects of the keywords which were not duplicated in the key image tags. For example, the *Guardian* keywords implied criticisms of the UK government's Prevent strategy and conveyed Muslims' views of the coronation of Charles III, while the key image tags did not indicate the presence of such stories. There is therefore value in comparing both images and text together, as a way of obtaining a fuller sense of the themes and representations associated with a newspaper corpus. However, so far, our analysis hasn't considered specifically how words and images combine together to make meaning. To do so, we need to carry out a multimodal analysis.

6.4 Stage 4: Multimodal Analysis of the Top Key Image Tags

In this section and in Section 6.5, we carry out multimodal analyses, bringing together the written text and images and considering how they work in concert to create meaning. There are two ways that we can approach this form of analysis. First, we can ask: which words tend to appear with particular kinds of images? Second, we can reverse the question, asking: which kinds of images tend to appear with particular words? In this section we will address the first question.

Table 7 shows the top key image tag for each newspaper and considers the words that are most likely to be associated with it. To do this, we carried out keyness comparisons based on the presence or absence of a particular image tag in a certain newspaper. For example, the top key image tag in the *Daily Mail* was Crowd (with 621 occurrences). In WordSmith we created a wordlist from a sub-corpus consisting just of *Daily Mail* articles that contained images that had been tagged as Crowd, and then compared it against a wordlist from a second sub-corpus consisting of *Daily Mail* articles that didn't contain any images tagged as Crowd.

Table 7 The top key image tag for each newspaper, with associated keywords and collocates

Newspaper	Top key image tag	Top keywords	Top lexical collocates	Top image collocates
Daily Mail	Crowd (621)	Gaza (600), Israeli (443), Hamas (528), Israel (568), city (315), council (375), Palestinian (306), Friday (251), Palestinians (174), protest (179)	Friday (118), people (56), Muslims (53), protesters (47), Sinead (43), Gaza (41), Palestinian (38), Palestinians (37), city (33), gather (29)	PublicEvent (498), City (358), Street (298), Hat (254), Pedestrian (218), Protest (188), Tree (119), Building (115), Sky (103), Cap (103)
Daily Star	Chest (131)	her (501), she (393), Mia (60), Knoll (58), BBC (50), I (376), brand (33), fans (83), Lee (37), was (468)	Mia (15), world (9), Knoll (9), Miss (8), Ivana (7), ex (7), Emery (6), year (6), Croatia (6), fan (5)	HumanLeg (78), Trunk (78), BlackHair (68), LongHair (65), Waist (63), Eyelash (46), Undergarment (44), Brassiere (43), Shoulder (38), Navel (38)
The Express	Tie (116)	party (87), Keir (68), Labour (87), his (285), Starmer (48), election (26), he (366), Sir (65), Corbyn (16), Mr (110)	Keir (9), Starmer (9), Sunak (7), Queen (6), Biden (6), war (6), Rishi (6), Rania (6), president (5), princess (5)	Speech (47), Employment (47), Collar (43), DressShirt (45), PublicSpeaking (39), PublicEvent (34), Smile (29), Chin (25), Beard (24), FacialHair (24)

The Guardian	Organ (13)	her (118), justice (35), Charles (33), King (46), Coronation (36), she (107), victims (19), someone (9), his (116), course (14), independent (11)	woman (2), prosecute (2), Eleanor (2), promotion (1), protest (1), save (1), pomp (1), met (1), Lucy (1), matters (1)	PortraitPhotography (8), Chin (8), Forehead (8), Ear (6), Eyelash (6), Eyebrow (6), Eye (6), Lip (6), Tie (6), Nose (6)
The Independent	Room (80)	murder (65), stabbed (38), mother (53), hate (90), son (41), crime (46), prayer (45), Palestinian (71), Hamas (71), old (56)	Fayoume (10), Wadea (9), Muslim (6), father (6), Ramadan (5), stabbing (5), family (4), Oday (4), Palestinian (4), Muslims (3)	Hat (22), Pattern (18), Employment (16), Cap (15), City (14), Plaid (13), Sleeve (12), Tartan (12), Crowd (11), Building (11)
The Mirror	Cuisine (29)	Ramadan (128), Eid (104), you (143), fast (44), food (42), day (61), Muslims (64), meal (23), is (9), month (52)	Ramdan (10), Eid (4), come (2), 2023 (2), people (2), families (2), experience (2), get (2), day (2), days (2), going (2)	Dish (26), Recipe (24), Plate (22), Cooking (21), Tableware (18), Table (17), Ingredient (11), Sharing (11), Food (9), FoodCraving (8)
The Sun	Gas (92)	hospital (170), rocket (111), Hamas (290), Israeli (177), Gaza (201), Israel (249),	hospital (15), Gaza (9), footage (9), Hamas (8), blast (7), killed (6), attack	Heat (39), Night (32), Sky (31), Pollution (30), Building (30), Darkness

Table 7 (cont.)

Newspaper	Top key image tag	Top keywords	Top lexical collocates	Top image collocates
		footage (81), IDF (87), missile (46), air (60)	(6), Israel (6), Israeli (5), released (5)	(29), Fire (29), City (28), Asphalt (24), Vehicle (24)
The Telegraph	Protest (76)	Palestine (84), anti (128), march (62), pro (65), protest (53), protesters (48), Jewish (74), Jews (64), Hamas (160), Semitic (37)	pro (13), protesters (10), Palestinian (9), Israel (6), march (5), Palestine (5), said (4), officers (4), demonstrators (4), met (4)	PublicEvent (76), Crowd (73), Hat (40), Tree (31), Pedestrian (31), Street (31), Sky (27), Jacket (27), City (27), Community (18)
The Times	Tie (180)	Gaza (358), Israel (414), Hamas (363), Labour (220), Palestinian (218), Yousaf (125), Israeli (214), Israel's (88), Starmer (119), party (210)	Starmer (10), Humza (10), Yousaf (10), minister (7), Keir (7), Hamas (6), right (6), president (6), Israel (5), Biden (5)	Speech (69), Employment (64), PublicEvent (62), DressShirt (62), PublicSpeaking (55), Collar (55), Smile (51), FacialHair (37), Beard (36), Moustache (36)

Then, the Advanced Settings were changed to specify that files should be selected 'Only if containing' the image tag under scrutiny (i.e. <xxxCrowd>). A wordlist was then created using only the files containing the chosen tag. Then in Advanced Settings, the tag was moved to the 'Must not contain'[5] section of the 'Only if containing' window, and a second wordlist was created. The two wordlists were then used to derive keywords. To do this, the default setting of mark-up to ignore <*> in WordSmith was left intact. The first wordlist was obtained by altering the Tag settings in WordSmith by selecting the option 'Only if containing' and entering the code <xxxCrowd> in one of the boxes under 'Must contain'. The second wordlist was obtained by moving <xxxCrowd> to one of the boxes under 'Must not contain'.[6]

As before, we listed the 10 keywords most strongly associated with the tag. We also considered the 10 highest-frequency lexical collocates of the image tag Crowd and its 10 highest image collocates. To find word collocates we first changed the Concordance settings from 'stop at sentence break' to 'no limits', and we altered both minimum frequency and minimum length to 1. We then carried out a concordance search on the tag (i.e. <xxxCrowd>) and clicked on the collocates tab to see its lexical collocates. To identify tags which collocated with other tags, we changed the default settings, removing <*> from 'mark-up to ignore' and changing the collocation span to L20 and R20 as well as specifying that collocates should 'stop at sentence break'.

As we are only focussing on the top key image tag for each newspaper, our findings can't be generalised to every image or every article but are instead focussed around the language associated with a particularly distinctive image tag for each newspaper. In looking at nine key tags in total in this way, we should be able to get a sense regarding the extent to which it is worthwhile carrying out this kind of analysis. While carrying out the analysis for each tag we asked: do the results tell us something new beyond what we already found out about this key tag and its associated words when we looked at them separately?

In order to carry out this part of the analysis, we examined concordances of the top 10 keywords associated with each top key image tag in each newspaper. Using the Image Tag Explorer tool we had created, we also examined the images for each newspaper that contained the top key image tag and, where it was useful to do so, we went back to the original news articles online in order to gain a better impression of how images and text interacted. While our analysis brought up a range of different kinds of findings, we have tried to prioritise those

---

[5] In earlier editions of WordSmith, the labels for these settings are different. For instance, WordSmith 9 has 'Must not contain', but WordSmith 7 has 'but not'.

[6] It should be noted that the tag settings were case-sensitive, so <xxxcrowd> or <XXXCROWD> would not have returned appropriate wordlists.

which addressed the central question of this analysis: in what ways do the text and images link to representations of Muslims and Islam?

We begin with the top key image tag in the *Daily Mail*, Crowd, which occurs in 26% of the *Daily Mail*'s images. One collocate of images tagged as Crowd is *Sinead*, which, as noted earlier, refers to images of crowds at the procession of Sinead O'Connor's funeral. Analysis of relevant concordance lines indicates that O'Connor's religion is described respectfully by the *Daily Mail*. For example:

> Shaykh Dr Umar Al-Qadri, chief Imam at the Islamic Centre of Ireland, told MailOnline that Sinead was to have a Muslim burial on [*sic*] accordance with her conversion to the religion, referring to her with her adopted name Shuhada Sadaqat. (*Daily Mail*, 8 August 2023)

Dr Al-Qadri is also given a 66-word quote in this article, referring to O'Connor's 'beautiful personality' and how her funeral reflected both her Irish and her Muslim identities. The article could be seen as a eulogy and is one of the most positive articles involving Islam in the *Daily Mail* corpus.

More typically though, the *Daily Mail* images tagged Crowd tend to occur in articles containing words which relate to the conflict between Israel and Hamas (*Gaza, Israeli, Hamas, Israel, Palestinian* and *Palestinians*). Such images tend to show scenes of protests or war devastation as a result of bombings and other forms of attack. The protests involve images of people burning Israeli flags, carrying posters which show the American president Joe Biden with a Hitler moustache or raising guns in the air. Other scenes show police restraining protesters. The war scenes are some of the most violently explicit in the corpus, showing people with injuries, being carried away on stretchers through rubble or setting fire to objects. One image is of a man holding an infant who has been badly injured. Text accompanying these kinds of images often describes *Hamas* in strongly negative terms:

> Dr Wahid Shaida, aka Abdul Wahid, pictured, celebrated the barbaric Hamas terror attacks that slaughtered 1,400 Jewish men. (*Daily Mail*, 28 October 2023)

> Another male in a grey hoodie held up a megaphone and appeared to continually bellow 'Hamas' in the 35-second clip which has had more than three million views on X. (*Daily Mail*, 22 October 2023)

Palestinians (as opposed to *Hamas*) do not receive the same level of negative representation, although they still tend to be associated with violence:

> A Palestinian uses a slingshot during clashes with Israeli soldiers at the north entrance of the Palestinian city of Ramallah, near Beit El Jewish settlement, in the occupied West Bank on Friday. (*Daily Mail*, 13 October 2023)

Palestinian Islamic Jihad militant group gunmen are seen in the West Bank. (*Daily Mail*, 28 November 2023)

Clashes with Palestinian security forces broke out in a number of other cities in the West Bank, which is ruled by Abbas' Palestinian Authority, late on Tuesday. (*Daily Mail*, 17 October 2023)

References to *Israel* which occur in the context of Crowd images tend to refer to actions by pro-Palestine protesters, which cast them negatively, as in the following excerpt, which describes the actor Susan Sarandon:

She attended another over the weekend, where she was seen chanting 'from the river to the sea,' which has been branded an anti-Semitic phrase that calls for the destruction of Israel. (*Daily Mail*, 21 November 2023)

Other references to Israel show events from a sympathetic perspective, particularly relating to the Israeli hostages. The following text excerpt accompanies an image tagged as Crowd:

Tal Goldstein-Almog, 9, (pictured) was seen being cradled by his loved ones after he and the other hostages arrived back in Israel. (*Daily Mail*, 28 November 2023)

Another keyword which occurs with articles containing Crowd images in the *Daily Mail* is *Friday*. Closer analysis of concordance lines indicates that this relates to descriptions of protests, marches and rallies occuring after Friday prayers around the world. In the following example, the water metaphor 'poured' represents Muslims as a single, uncontrollable mass:

crowds of Muslim worshippers poured into the streets after weekly Friday prayers, angered by devastating Israeli airstrikes on Gaza. (*Daily Mail*, 13 October 2023)

In the next example, former leader of Hamas Khal is described as calling for a Day of Jihad on Friday:

Khaled Meshaal, the former leader of Hamas, is pictured in October 2018 in Istanbul. He has called for a 'Day of Jihad' on Friday, in a statement released from Qatar, where he now lives. (*Daily Mail*, 13 October 2023)

Analysis of the relationship between images tagged as Crowd and accompanying text in the *Daily Mail* shows a mixed picture then. There is respectful reporting around the funeral of Sinead O'Connor, who was a Muslim, but there are other representations of Muslims as angry and anti-Semitic when protesting about the Israel–Hamas conflict.

As we have seen, many of the images in the *Daily Star* are of female models, including the majority of those tagged with the top key image tag Chest, attrributed to 22% of the newpaper's images. These images tend to occur in articles which show models defying expectations associated with women in Islam by being sexually provocative, hence the keywords *her, she, Mia* and *Knoll*. The keyword *brand* relates to adult film star Mia Khalifa's jewellery brand Sheytan. Additionally, the first-person pronoun *I* occurs as a keyword with articles containing images tagged as Chest. We have already seen how the keyword *I* indicated that *Daily Star* articles were more likely to give personal perspectives. However, the fact that *I* also occurs as a keyword more specifically for *Daily Star* articles containing images tagged as Chest tells us more clearly that such personal perspectives tend to be associated with the women shown in those pictures. In the following example, former Miss Croatia Ivana Knoll (whose image is tagged as Chest 23 times) is quoted as reacting to the dress code in Qatar when she attends the World Cup:

> 'I heard about the rules and I was shocked,' she told PA. 'The dress code forbids showing shoulders, knees, belly and everything and I was like "Oh my God, I don't even have the clothes to cover all of that".' (*Daily Star*, 2 December 2022)

The keyword *fans* also occurs as part of these stories, with articles describing how Knoll displayed her body at a football match in Qatar. However, other articles with pictures tagged Chest containing *fans* and *BBC* relate to a 1999 documentary about football hooligans, including 'Britain's most infamous football hooligan', Jason Marriner, who is described as being involved in violence with rival fans. Marriner is also said to have a freezer with an image of Lee Rigby on it (hence the keyword *Lee*), a fusilier who was murdered in a terror attack by a Muslim. The *Daily Star* doesn't represent Marriner sympathetically, noting that he made Nazi salutes at Auschwitz, and an accompanying image shows Marriner, unsmiling, with tattooed arms folded across his chest. Chiefly though, the *Daily Star* uses images tagged as Chest to represent Islam as restricting women who want to show off their bodies.

As noted earlier, in the *Express*, the Tie tag tends to be assigned to images of male political figures. One top-10 keyword associated with Tie, *election*, refers to recent elections in the Netherlands, Finland, France and the European Parliament. Articles about the Dutch election feature photographs of (tie-wearing) candidate Geert Wilders, leader of the far-right Party for Freedom, with Wilders being described as having 'toned down some of his anti-Islam viewpoints'. However, an analysis of the other nine keywords associated with *Express* articles containing images tagged as Tie found a focus on two men, Sir Keir Starmer and Mr Jeremy Corbyn, respectively the incumbent leader of the Labour Party and his predecessor. The male pronoun keywords *he* and *his* typically refer to Keir Starmer. Although Corbyn is mentioned in some articles containing pictures tagged as Tie, he typically is not shown in the accompanying pictures; we only found two pictures of him, and both of these also featured Starmer.

The *Express* images of Starmer which are tagged as Tie do not particularly represent him in a positive light. Although he is wearing a suit, he is shown with shadows around his eyes, unsmiling or with his mouth open while talking. We examined the images in the *Express* which contained both the Tie and Smile tags, finding that they mostly involved pictures of members of the British royal family although politicians like Geert Wilders, Humza Yousaf, Vladimir Putin and Rishi Sunak are also pictured wearing ties and smiling. Keir Starmer appeared in three of these Tie + Smile images, although it was another person who was smiling, not Starmer. On the whole the Tie images which occur in articles about Starmer look like images that are taken by a press photographer or screenshots from news broadcasts as opposed to publicity images that would have been posed and carefully chosen to show him in a good light.

A concordance analysis of *Starmer* in articles containing photos tagged Tie indicates how the Labour Party leader is negatively represented. This is achieved in two ways. First, he is described as not being in control: 'hit by the biggest rebellion of his leadership'; 'lost control of the narrative'; 'a prisoner of his own party'; 'locked in crisis talks'; 'caving to pressure'. Second, he is seen as causing division and anger, particularly among Muslims: 'sparking fury'; 'accused of gas-lighting Muslims'; 'criticised by Imam'; 'rumbled after turning up to mosque uninvited'. The unflattering photographs of Starmer act in collaboration with the negative textual representations of him, suggesting an *Express* campaign to persuade readers not to support Labour in advance of the coming general election. Within this, articles about Starmer's relationship with Muslims appear to be a useful means to an end, although they also contribute to a well-established press representation of Muslims as involved in conflict.

The *Guardian*'s strongest key image tag, Organ, is quite rare, appearing only 13 times (and in just 6% of the *Guardian*'s images), so we shouldn't overstate any claims about its generalisability. Organ always occurred in images involving faces (11 out of 13 are in close-ups), which helps explain the presence of other tags like Eye, Ear and Chin in these images. The majority of these images (11 out of 13) are not of Muslims. The tag appears in images alongside articles that have a high number of third-person pronouns (associated keywords being *his*, *her* and *she*). Five of the Organ-tagged images are of young women, and further analysis indicates that they are of Eleanor Williams, a woman who falsely claimed she had been trafficked by a gang of Asian men, and Lucy Letby, a nurse who was convicted of killing seven babies and attempting to kill six others. The Williams case initially inspired a Facebook group called Justice for Ellie (hence the keyword *justice* appearing in *Guardian* articles containing Organ pictures), while articles describe her as in court for perverting the course of justice (also explaining *course* and *justice* as keywords). Articles also describe how her claims resulted in Muslims being victimised:

> It set off a chain of events that included a far-right group gaining a foothold in Barrow, and drove a sharp rise in racism and Islamophobia. Curry house windows were smashed, beloved restaurants were boycotted and one Muslim takeaway owner was chased down the street by men who poured alcohol over his head. (*The Guardian*, 1 March 2023)

The Lucy Letby case involves a quote from a Muslim woman, whose sister was murdered in 2021. Similar to the outcome of Letby's trial, the murderer refused to come into the court for sentencing, and the *Guardian* provides quotes from the Muslim woman who is campaigning for the law to be changed.

Three images tagged Organ in the *Guardian* involve pictures of King Charles III, and as seen earlier, the *Guardian* wrote about Muslims in relationship to Charles' coronation (with *Charles*, *coronation* and *king* being keywords for articles containing Organ images). Further investigation of relevant articles indicated that King Charles was represented as having positive views on Islam:

> Charles's own faith is 'deep and strong, but more questing, more intellectual, more complex' than his mother's, said Ian Bradley, an emeritus professor of cultural and spiritual history at the University of St Andrews and the author of God Save the King: The Sacred Nature of the Monarch. 'He's clearly drawn to eastern Orthodox Christianity and aspects of Islam. He's interested in all kinds of spirituality.' (*The Guardian*, 4 May 2023)

The multimodal analysis of the Organ image tag found that while there were a variety of images associated with the tag, they involved the *Guardian* taking a positive stance towards Islam – casting Muslims as victims of injustice or focussing on Charles III as respectful towards Islam.

The key image tag Room appears in 17% of *Independent* images and tends to also occur in articles which have words relating to crime as keywords: *murder*, *stabbed*, *hate* and *crime*. An analysis of Room images which appear with these keywords indicates that 13 of them are of a young boy wearing a hat with the words 'Happy Birthday' on it. (Hat is the strongest tag collocate of Room for the *Independent* images.) Other images contain a picture of an informally dressed, bearded man who appears to be at a press conference. In some pictures he is being consoled by other people. Analysis of concordance lines shows that these images are from articles about a six-year-old Muslim boy from a town near Chicago who was murdered in an anti-Muslim hate crime while trying to hug his landlord, described as 'a man radicalised by right-wing radio reports about Israel–Hamas'. The boy's mother was also stabbed multiple times in the attack. These articles present ordinary Muslims sympathetically and provide numerous quotes from family members of the boy, such as the following:

> Odey Al-Fayoume, the father of Wadea Al-Fayoume, said in a speech in Arabic outside his son's funeral. 'I'm here as the father of a boy whose rights were violated.' Wadea was stabbed 26 times at the family's home in Plainfield Township, outside Chicago, on Saturday morning, exactly a week after the conflict overseas erupted. 'The issue of Hamas and Gaza is an issue of people, not countries', Mr Al-Fayoume said, according to the Associated Press. (*The Independent*, 16 October 2023)

Two other sets of *Independent* articles containing images tagged as Room also involve Muslims who are targets of (possible) hate crimes. However, a third set involved a story about a gay teenager who was murdered by a group of men at a gas station in Brooklyn. A witness claimed the men who attacked the teenager 'allegedly said they were Muslims'. All four attacks took place in the US, and while it is not unusual for broadsheet newspapers to focus on international stories, it seems that the *Independent* has a particular interest in hate crimes involving American Muslims, usually as innocent victims.

The *Mirror*'s top key image tag, Cuisine, occurs 29 times (in 3% of *Mirror* images), and it often appears with other food-related tags like Dish, Recipe, Cooking and Plate. Twenty images involve multiple people (usually Muslim families, including parents and children) sharing numerous dishes of food around a table. These images also occur in articles that contain words relating to *Ramadan* (also *Eid*, *fast*, *food*, *Muslims*, *meal* and *month*), as described earlier. The text associated with these articles tends to be informational while focussing on the positive aspects of Ramadan:

> Scientific studies have shown that fasting provides several health benefits 'Muslims around the world fast during daylight hours, meaning they abstain from eating, drinking or engaging in sexual relations for the duration of their fast.' (*The Mirror*, 21 February 2023)

> 'But sometimes there is this misconception that we as Muslim's are struggling during Ramadan and need pity. For me, it's actually the opposite – being able to practice Ramadan together with family and friends makes it a very enjoyable experience and one I look forward to every year.' (*The Mirror*, 19 April 2023)

The Mirror therefore represents Ramadan as a positive aspect of Islam, with Cuisine-tagged images reinforcing aspects of the representation which depict it as a sociable and enjoyable family occasion.

In the *Sun*, the top key image tag is Gas, which occurs in 6% of *Sun* images. It tends to appear in articles that contain words relating to the Israel–Hamas conflict, relating to those involved (*Hamas*, *Israeli*, *Gaza*, *Israel* and *IDF*), weapons (*rocket*, *missile* and *air* (strikes)), casualties (*hospital*) and coverage of the conflict (*footage*). As we have already seen, our analysis of *Sun* keywords like *rocket* and *hospital* revealed that there was often a negative representation of Hamas and Muslims, with *rocket* and *hospital* being chiefly used to refer to a rocket launched by Islamic Jihad (an ally of Hamas) which misfired and destroyed a hospital in Gaza. The text accompanying photos tagged Gas can be quite horrific (a content warning is given for the following example):

> Horror footage from the hospital showed the blaze engulfing the building, with the hospital's grounds littered with bodies, many of them young children. Blood-soaked sheets covering a huge pile of victims could be seen across what was left of the hospital's grounds, as witnesses say the 'smell of bodies' now hangs in the air. (*The Sun*, 18 October 2023)

The accompanying images tagged as Gas chiefly show pictures of buildings on fire or of missiles being fired. Only a small minority of these images contain people, although two show people carrying injured children, amid bombed buildings. A closer examination of some articles indicates that they contain photos of both Israeli and Palestinian children. However, the text in these articles appears to give a more negative representation towards Hamas as opposed to the IDF, with more quotes being critical of Hamas. This is a case where the images do not fully reflect the content of the text. Perhaps this is because such images might have been difficult for journalists to obtain. However, it is also likely that the images would not be printed, even if they had been obtained, because they would be much too distressing for newspaper audiences to see. Instead, the focus on images of explosions gives evidence of the scale of devastation that took place, while the accompanying texts provide a mental image of the effects on the population.

In the *Telegraph*, the top key image tag, Protest, occurs in images relating to pro-Palestine marches and protests about attacks on it. Concordance analysis of keywords associated with articles containing these images, like *protesters*, *anti*, *Jews* and *Hamas*, indicates that the *Telegraph* is concerned about the protests. For example, in one article the *Telegraph* quotes concerns from numerous people, including the UK's counter-extremism commissioner, Robin Simcox, a former independent reviewer of terrorism legislation, Lord Carlile, and the head of the review of the anti-radicalisation programme Prevent, William Shawcross. In another article the *Telegraph* reports on the Metropolitan Police's decision not to arrest protesters who shout 'jihad' on marches, quoting Commander Kyle Gordon who, said that there are a myriad of circumstances in which someone may use the word. The literal meaning of jihad is struggle, or effort. It can refer to a believer's internal struggle to live out their Muslim faith and to build a good Muslim society, and it can also refer to holy war. (*The Telegraph*, 27 October 2023)

At the end of this article, there is a report of the numbers of anti-Semitic and Islamophobic offences (408 and 174), arrests (75), police visits to vulnerable premises (4,960), counter-terror investigations (10), counter-terror referrals (1,500) and live terror investigations (10). One interpretation of these statistics is that they are used to raise concern about terror and violence, implicitly criticising the decision not to arrest people who shout 'jihad' on pro-Palestine marches.

One of the most complex images in the corpus is one tagged Protest in the *Telegraph* which appears at the start of an opinion column entitled 'How Labour is tearing itself apart over Gaza'. The image comprises a red rectangle, where a strip has been roughly ripped across the middle part, revealing a black and white photograph of a pro-Palestine protest with people holding signs. In the foreground, a figure wearing a burka (which shows only eyes) appears to be holding up a clenched fist. The use of red in the image could be interpreted in several ways. Red can mean danger or it can symbolise blood, suggesting violence. Also, red is the colour associated with the Labour Party, so the image could be interpreted as metaphor, showing a Labour Party flag which is being literally torn apart by the protests. The image therefore could be seen as trying to raise concern about both the pro-Palestinian protesters and the Labour Party.

However, the main impression gained from reading articles about the protests is one of concern about Muslims engaging in anger and hate. The pictures work in concert with the text in the *Telegraph* articles which express concern about the protests as fomenting hate and leading to violence and terror.

As with the *Express*, the key image tag for the *Times* is Tie, which tends to show images of men in suits, especially politicians. According to the Cloud Vision Release Notes, in February 2020, a decision was made to remove gendered labels like man and woman, as gender cannot be inferred by appearance and use of such labels would not align with Google's Artificial Intelligence Principle to avoid creating or reinforcing unfair bias.[7] However, a key tag like Tie might imply that men are relatively over-represented in a particular corpus, especially as this tag co-occurs with FacialHair, Beard and Moustache. Two sets of keywords co-occur with Tie images in the *Times*. First, there are keywords relating to the Israel–Hamas conflict (*Gaza, Israel, Hamas, Palestinian, Israel*

---

[7] https://cloud.google.com/vision/docs/release-notes#February_19_2020.

and *Israel's*), and second, there are keywords relating to British politics (*Labour, Yousaf* and *party*). These two sets of words are actually related, though, in that the *Times* discusses the conflict through the lens of British politics, particularly focussing on the Labour's party response to it (similarly to the *Express*).

Analysis of these keywords in context indicates that, compared to the other newspapers, the *Times* is less likely to write articles about Muslims to attack Labour, or to criticise pro-Palestinian protests. For example, in one article, Labour MPs are described as having given security advice after receiving threats 'amid the Israel and Gaza tensions'. Starmer is described in relatively positive terms as moving 'to calm tensions in his party', and the article quotes a 'Labour source', suggesting that the newspaper has connections to Labour Party members. As with the *Express*, some images tagged Tie are of Keir Starmer, but unlike the *Express*, these images tend to show him more positively, surrounded by supporters, meeting with Muslim and Jewish communities and smiling while making a speech. An article entitled 'Four hard lessons Keir Starmer must learn from Labour's Gaza split' offers the Labour leader advice and ends by stating that Starmer will be the next prime minister. An image of Starmer shows him in close-up with members of his shadow cabinet in the background. The image also contains red stripes and a red rose, symbols of the Labour Party, with a similar use of red to that of the *Telegraph* image analyzed in the preceding paragraphs. As noted previously, in the election the following year, the *Times* did not support any political party, which perhaps explains the more considered representations of Labour and Keir Starmer in these articles.

6.5 Stage 5: Multimodal Analysis of the Top Keyword in Each Newspaper

In the second part of the multimodal analysis, we begin not with a key image tag but with a keyword. Here we ask the questions: what image tags co-occur with a particular keyword in the same article? and how do the images in these articles work in conjunction with the keyword to represent Muslims and Islam? Table 8 shows the top keyword for each newspaper, along with their top lexical collocates, as well as the key image tags (and their collocating image tags) associated with articles which contain those keywords. Although it was not planned or predicted, the nine top keywords (*council, her, remembrance, UK, Muslim, Ramadan, cops, Mr* and *writes*) come from diverse part-of-speech categories: one pronoun, one title, one verb, three nouns and three kinds of proper nouns. It is therefore interesting to compare the kinds of image tags they attract and the

Table 8 The top keyword for each newspaper, with associated collocates and image tags

Newspaper	Top keyword	Top lexical collocates	Top 10 key image tags	Top image collocates
Daily Mail	council (421)	Cllr (366), city (132), Birmingham (61), borough (58), member (51), cabinet (47), Khan (44), Hussain (36), Muslim (31), Newham (30)	Tie (41), Employment (29), DressShirt (27), Room (27), Moustache (22)	Tie (10), Employment (8), Window (8), PublicEvent (7), DressShirt (6), FacialHair (6), Interaction (6), Crowd (5), Smile (5), Trousers (4)
Daily Star	her (637)	fans (18), first (18), husband (18), new (18), death (17), body (17), name (16), career (16), outfits (16), home (15)	Waist (89), LongHair (97), BlackHair (96), Lip (59), Undergarment (48), Blond (47), Beauty (47), Eyelash (82), PortraitPhotography (91), Brassiere (51)	Smile (69), HumanLeg (68), Chest (59), Waist (58), BlackHair (55), Trunk (54), LongHair (48), Eyelash (38), Sleeve (38), PortraitPhotography (37)
The Express	remembrance (39)	day (16), Sunday (7), march (6), events (4), protect (4), weekend (4), Rowley (3), national (3), celebrations (3), Whitehall (2)	Black (2), Tie (11), Jacket (5), Protest (7), Human (5), Collar (7), Crowd (11), Chin (6), PublicEvent (12), People (3)	Cap (1), City (1), Face (1), Outerwear (1), Pattern (1), Pedestrian (1), Protest (1), PublicEvent (1), Street (1)

Table 8 (cont.)

Newspaper	Top keyword	Top lexical collocates	Top 10 key image tags	Top image collocates
The Guardian	UK (227)	government (16), said (13), headlines (9), sign (8), government's (7), Israel (7), allowed (7), civilian 6), return (6), foreign (6)	Wood (7), Product (6), Engineering (5), Line (5), Rectangle (5), StepCutting (5), Tie (24), Pattern (15)	Speech (6), FacialHair (6), Tie (5), Employment (4), PublicEvent (4), Moustache (4), Jaw (3), PortraitPhotography (3), Metal (3), Smile (3)
The Independent	Muslim (833)	anti (58), said (51), women (46), communities (43), community (37), world (32), first (27), countries (26), Jewish (25), hate (23)	Car (25), AutomotiveExterior (24), PublicSpace (23), HeadGear (18), Road (60)	PublicEvent (28), City (26), Room (25), Uniform (19), Street (19), PortraitPhotography (18), Crowd (16), Road (16), Pedestrian (14), Moustache (14)
The Mirror	Ramadan (258)	month (41), fasting (25), end (22), Muslims (17), year (14), time (11), holy (9), observing (9), days (8), Eid (7)	Plate (22), Cuisine (26), Food (28), Tableware (25), Dish (23), Recipe (21), Table (20), Cooking (19), Sharing (15), Ingredient (12)	Room (23), Smile (17), Table (15), Dish (14), Cuisine (13), Plate (13), Pattern (12), Tableware (12), Cooking (12), Recipe (11)

The Sun	cops (86)	terror (8), attack (8), arrested (7), shot (6), probe (6), man (5), said (4), launch (3), Islamist (3), jihadi (3)	AutomotiveLighting (32), Beard (55), ModeOfTransport (45), FacialHair (51), Wheel (40), EmergencyService (4), Security (16), EmergencyVehicle (5), Tire (39)	Pedestrian (10), Street (9), Darkness (8), Uniform (7), Sky (7), Road (7), Crowd (7), Room (7), City (7), PublicEvent (6)
The Telegraph	Mr (479)	said (109), Wilders (32), Yousaf (28), Malik (17), told (16), Netanyahu (15), added (14), Shawcross (14), Hall (13), Ramadan (12)	Tie (60), Thumb (6), Interaction (9), DressShirt (31), VehicleRegistrationPlate (7), PersonalLuxuryCar (7), Standing (7), Employment (35)	Tie (10), PublicEvent (9), Room (6), Employment (6), Beard (6), Sky (5), Protest (5), Community (5), Crowd (5), FacialHair (5)
The Times	writes (66)	Abbie (7), Cheeseman (7), said (5), Acheson (4), David (4), Lucinda (4), Joshua (3), Khan (3), Kieran (3), Thurston (3)	FlagOfTheUnitedStates (9), HighVisibilityClothing (11), Atmosphere (5), Pollution (10), Podium (8), Security (12), Car (15), Horizon (7), Night (17), LandVehicle (5)	AutomotiveWheelSystem (1), Circle (1), Cloud (1), Friendship (1), Glasses (1), Grass (1), Iris (1), Sky (1), Smile (1), Symbol (1)

extent to which the analysis of each newspaper reveals something new about its representation of Muslims and Islam.

We derived the keyword lists as outlined in Sections 6.4 but typed the relevant keyword rather than a key image tag into the 'Only if containing' boxes. To obtain the most frequent image tag collocates we used the same procedure as outlined in Section 6.4, although we removed <*> from 'mark-up to ignore' and we also changed the collocation horizons to -20 and +20. The mean number of tags per image was 10.42, although some images had 20 tags. Widening the collocation horizons meant that we were able to obtain all the tag collocates of a word.

In the *Daily Mail*, the top keyword, *council*, occurs 421 times across 51 articles, although in terms of distribution, two articles (published on the same day) each account for 150 occurrences. As described earlier, these articles both describe how the Labour Party leader Keir Starmer's stance on Gaza resulted in criticism from some Labour Party councillors, who signed an open letter to him. Both articles contain the letter with all of the signatories listed at the end. These articles show pictures of Starmer and other politicians speaking in parliament, and explain, to an extent, the presence of key image tags like Tie, DressShirt and Employment.

Other uses of *council* refer to American councils or groups and involve stories which represent Muslims as having influence in various ways. For example, Minneapolis City Council is described as allowing broadcasts of the Muslim call to prayer, and the *Daily Mail* notes that 'the decision drew no organised community opposition'. Articles about Hamtramck City Council describe it as having an all-Muslim government which has banned LGBT pride flags on business and residential properties, and also 'voted to allow religious animal sacrifices in the home'. These articles detail opposition to Hamtramck City Council, quoting people who do not agree with the changes.

Not all articles imply that Muslims in America are being unreasonable. For example, the *Daily Mail* reports on a story about a Minnesota university professor who was fired after a student complained she had shown students an image of Prophet Mohammad. However, the Muslim Public Affairs Council is quoted as saying that the professor should be reinstated. Another article, about the Council on American Islamic Relations, describes the group as defending a student who was criticised by her university for accusing Israelis of 'settler colonialism'. Images which appear with articles with the word *council* contain photographs of Muslims in formal dress making podium speeches at press conferences or council meetings. An article from 15 June 2023 about the banning of pride flags shows pictures of male council members who are Muslims (tagged as Moustache, Tie, DressShirt and Employment) at a meeting where non-Muslims (dressed more informally) protest against the flag ban. An interpretation of such image tags is that they help to signify the power and maleness of the decision-makers in contrast to the other members of the community. Another potential interpretation of these articles is that they function as a warning to British readers about the potential removal of rights if Muslims gain positions of power.

The top *Daily Star* keyword, *her*, occurred 637 times in that newspaper across 64 out of 101 articles. As we have seen, the *Daily Star* has a relatively high number of articles about female models with accompanying photographs. Such women are described as having fans, and there are references to them having an 'adult career'. In the following excerpt, one model is described as dealing with death threats:

> Her strict Muslim upbringing has seen her deal with death threats. Recalling the moment when her mum found out about her adult career, she said: 'When she found out, she was devastated and heartbroken'. (*Daily Star*, 3 June 2023)

The image tags attributed to images in articles containing the word *her* tend to relate to glamour models (e.g. Undergarment, Brassiere, Beauty, Waist and LongHair). It is notable that Smile and PortraitPhotography occur as image tag collocates (i.e. in images that occur in the vicinity of the word *her*), indicating that these images were taken by professional photographers and that they represent the models positively, with a happy appearance. By implication, Islam is framed as a repressive religion, restricting the choices of women who want to model (and anyone who wants to look at them).

All the uses of the top *Express* keyword, *remembrance*, refer to Remembrance Day. As we have seen earlier, the *Express* reported on concerns that protests would be timed to coincide with Remembrance Day events or that there would be boycotts of them. In these articles, the *Express* quotes people who are supportive of Remembrance Day, such as Colonel Richard Kemp, who says

> 'it is worth remembering many Muslims as well as Christians, Jews and members of other religions, or no religion, fought and died for the freedom and liberty we enjoy today'. (*The Express*, 2 November 2023)

Additionally, the newspaper reports on calls to sack police chief Mark Rowley, who didn't ask for emergency powers to stop pro-Palestinian marches during the weekend when Remembrance Day occurred. In foregrounding such views, the *Express* implicitly appears to side with the view that the protest marches should not go ahead.

The image tags which appear in images in corresponding articles with the word *remembrance* tend to involve either pictures of people at Remembrance

Day events (e.g. Crowd, Black, Tie, Jacket and Collar) or images of people involved in protests relating to the conflict between Israel and Hamas (e.g. Crowd and Protest). We observed a difference between the two kinds of images. For example, one of the Tie images is a sombre picture of the incumbent prime minister together with one future and three past prime ministers (Liz Truss, Theresa May, Kier Starmer, Boris Johnson and Rishi Sunak) at a memorial event, all smartly dressed in black and wearing poppies (the men also in black ties), standing in front of two wreaths also made of poppies (Figure 8). One of the Crowd images, printed four days later, is of a policeman's fist against the side of a protester's face while people wearing face masks look on (Figure 9). The first image conveys a sense of dignity and reverence to the Remembrance Day events, while the protests are represented as a site of chaos and anger.

In the *Guardian*, the top keyword, *UK*, tends to occur with references to the British government and its relationship to other countries. For example, there are stories which relate to the status of asylum seekers from places like Sudan, stories relating to the government's stance on Shamina Begum, who left the UK in 2015 when she was 15 to join the Islamic State in Syria and lost her UK citizenship, and stories about the UK's role in the bombing campaign against Islamic State. These articles foreground voices critical of the government, for example:

Figure 8 Image in the *Express* (3 November 2023) showing past, present and future British prime ministers at a Remembrance Day event in London, tagged with Crowd, Black, Tie and Cap.

Figure 9 Image in the *Express* (7 November 2023) of a pro-Palestine march in London in an article about Remembrance Day, tagged with Crowd, Face, Cap, Human, Jacket and PublicEvent.

The government decision to revoke Begum's British citizenship – upheld last week by a special tribunal – has been condemned by a former supreme court justice. (*The Guardian*, 27 February 2023)

The key image tags for *UK* in the *Guardian* are somewhat unusual compared to the other sets of key image tags in Table 8, as only two of them relate to human beings (Tie and StepCutting). The most frequent key tag, Tie, tends to appear with images of politicians, whereas StepCutting relates to a multi-layered women's hairstyle (and occurs with images of Shamina Begum).

The other key image tags refer to abstract concepts, shapes or materials: Wood, Product, Engineering, Line, Rectangle and Pattern. The tags Line, Pattern and Rectangle appear in images of stamps and relate to an article about four new stamps that mark King Charles' coronation:

The diversity and community stamp, reflecting the multi-faith community and cultural diversity of Britain, features figures representing the Jewish, Islamic, Christian, Sikh, Hindu and Buddhist religions, and is representative of all faiths and none. (*The Guardian*, 28 April 2023)

Although we have seen how the *Guardian* was critical of King Charles, noting protests around his coronation, the stamps are written about in a positive way, indicating the more nuanced evaluative reporting style in the *Guardian*, which represents the UK as a diverse set of communities.

In the *Independent*, the top keyword, *Muslim,* is often used to refer to collective numbers of Muslims or locations where there are large number of Muslims (e.g. *communities, community, world* and *countries*). To an extent, this reflects the more international focus of broadsheet newspapers more generally. The collocates *anti* and *hate* are used in *Independent* articles which report on negative feeling towards Muslims (with the phrase *anti-Muslim hate* appearing 21 times). The word *first* collocates with *Muslim* and is used in reporting new developments, typically cases where Muslims are taking on roles or being involved in activities for the first time. For example, there are references to the first Muslim woman on Manchester City Council, Scotland's first Muslim leader and the first Muslim woman to lead an LGBTQ+ pride march (see Figure 10).

Similarly, the references to Muslim *women* report them as breaking boundaries – forming a running club or making World Cup history, as well as being subject to prejudice by conversative voices or attacked in terror incidents. The following excerpt contains a quote from an attendee of an Islamic convention being held in the UK, which emphasises the diversity of Muslims.

> Sarah Ward, a 43-year-old primary school teacher from Kingston, south-west London, said it is 'really nice' to see the diversity of the Muslim community as well as the unity that comes with the convention. 'We know, as Muslim

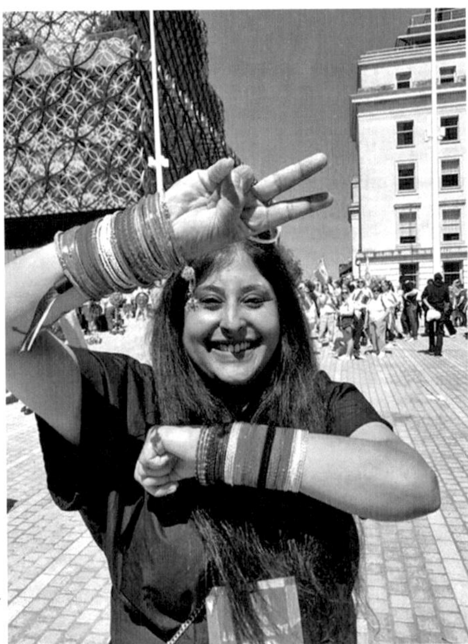

Figure 10 Image in the *Independent* (26 June 2023) of Saima Razzaq, the first Muslim woman to lead a LGBTQ+ pride march in Britain.

women, we're very diverse, we're not monolith, we're from different back-grounds, we have different skills, we have different passions, we do different jobs, but we come together as one community,' the mother-of-three told PA. (*The Independent*, 29 July 2023)

Of the image tags which are key in articles containing the word *Muslim*, the tags Car, AutomotiveExterior and Road tend to belong to pictures of cars, several of which come from an article which shows CCTV footage relating to a crime where a Muslim man was set on fire as he walked home from a mosque. Another image is from a crime scene where two Muslim women were stabbed to death at a Muslim centre in Portugal. A third is from a story about a disabled Muslim man who was beaten to death in Delhi after eating at a Hindu temple, and a fourth shows CCTV footage of a Muslim woman being attacked with a concrete slab by a stranger. These images are connected to stories of Muslims as victims of hate crimes. The cars are somewhat incidental to the images as they appear in CCTV footage which helps to provide evidence of the crimes being committed, in some cases shocking readers with the impact of seeing the crime as it is being carried out. *Independent* articles therefore tend to focus on sympathetic and diverse representations of Muslims, particularly showing participation of Muslim women in politics and sport or Muslims as victims of crime.

We have already seen how the keyword *Ramadan* in the *Mirror* (258 occur-rences) tends to be used in stories which tell readers about Ramadan and the practices associated with it for ordinary Muslims. This explains collocates like *fasting, observing, days, month, year, holy* and *Muslims*, as well as the food- and meal-related image tags associated with such articles. One image tag which collocates near the word *Ramadan* is Smile (occurring 17 times), and further examination of these images indicates that they show pictures of Muslim families, sitting around tables, sharing meals while smiling (see Figure 11 for an example). The text accompanying these Smile-tagged images presents a picture of the positives and negatives of the experience. Examples include: 'Many of us experience broken sleep in Ramadan'; 'I used to hide my period during Ramadan'; 'getting through the day can be a struggle at times'; 'The month is also a chance for Muslims to increase their prayers and give to charity as well as having many social gatherings for Iftar parties'. While the text sometimes presents Ramadan as challenging, the images enhance the positive representation of Ramadan as a form of worship, celebration and community for Muslims.

In the *Sun*, the top keyword, *cops* (86 occurrences), occurs with stories about suspected Islamist terror attacks, describing actions carried out by the police, such as shooting a suspect, launching a probe, interrogating someone or making an arrest. The key image tags associated with articles containing the word *cops*

Figure 11 A Muslim family smiling during Ramadan in the *Mirror* (21 February 2023). Image tags: Food, Smile, Tableware, Table, Sharing, Plate, Cuisine, Window, Cooking, Dish, Hat and Room.

are from images that show ambulances, fire engines and police cars attending crime scenes (e.g. AutomotiveLighting, ModeofTransport, Wheel, EmergencyService, Security, EmergencyVehicle and Tire). Two related tags – Beard and FacialHair – tend to be used in mug shots of male suspects or men convicted of the crimes in the stories, such as terrorists Abdesalem Lassoued and Usman Khan, would-be terrorist Matthew King and preacher Anjem Choudary (as in the following headline):

> Hate preacher Anjem Choudary quizzed by anti-terror cops who fear an Islamist attack sparked by Prince Harry. (*The Sun*, 4 May 2023)

Some mug shots or images are of men who have carried out hate crimes towards Muslims, including Darren Osborne, who killed one Muslim and injured nine more people when he drove a van into a mosque, or Jamie Barrow, who killed a Muslim family in an arson attack after an argument about household waste disposal. The images in these articles therefore show the identifiable faces of Muslim men who have been convicted of crimes, as well as men who have carried out crimes against Muslims. While Muslims are not always represented as criminals in these articles (as they are sometimes the victims), the overwhelming picture is a sense of Muslims being connected to violent crime in some way.

The *Telegraph*'s top keyword, *Mr* (479 occurrences), indicates a stylistic feature of this newspaper, in that it uses honorifics to refer to people. Of all the top keywords examined in this section, *Mr* is the only one which also appears in the top 10 keywords of other newspapers, also being in the lists for the *Independent* and the *Express*. The *Telegraph*'s style guide says 'Generally: at first mention use the person's name in full. Then use Mr, Mrs, Miss . . . '.[8] The rule does not apply to sports players, actors and entertainers, while doctors, professors, the clergy, police officers, nobility and members of the army are given specific titles. Collocates of *Mr* include surnames (*Wilders, Yousaf, Malik, Netanyahu, Shawcross* and *Hall*) as well as verbs of speech like *said, told* and *added*. The term of address tends to be especially used when quoting people, and usually occurs later in articles, after the person's full name has been given. For example, *Benjamin Netanyahu* occurs 25 times in the *Telegraph*, and in five cases (20%), he is described as making some sort of statement, through phrases like 'declaring the country to be at war', 'issued his own statement of response' and 'has pledged to crush Hamas'. On the other hand, there are 14 instances of *Mr Netanyahu*, seven (50%) of which involve him speaking. There are several possible interpretations of the *Telegraph*'s use of *Mr*. It makes references to people appear formal, respectful and distant, as well as giving an appearance of equality (for those who do not hold titles like Dr or Professor). For example, Vladimir Putin is referred to as *Mr Putin* as opposed to *President Putin*, as he is called in other newspapers. *Mr* is also a convention associated with Anglo culture. As the *Telegraph*'s style guide notes, 'We extend the Mr/Mrs rule to all foreigners: Mr Sarkozy, Mrs Merkel, Miss Dati'. The term is somewhat old-fashioned. Baker (2023: 419), for example, notes that preceding nouns of title like *Mr* show the greatest decline over time (in general written British English between 1931 and 2021) of any grammatical category.

There are two types of images associated with *Mr*. First, they are of male professionals. Closer examination of the collocating tags Tie, DressShirt, Employment and Interaction indicates that they are of political leaders from around the world, giving speeches or interacting with other people. However, the collocating tags Protest, Sky Crowd and Community are from images of protests. In such cases, there are quotes from politicians commenting chiefly on the Israel–Hamas conflict, for example:

> 'Those Arab countries who wish to establish diplomatic relations with the Zionist regime must now take a lesson from what has happened and think twice before doing so,' Mr Velayati told the Syrian foreign minister in a call on Monday. (*The Telegraph*, 9 October 2023)

---

[8] www.telegraph.co.uk/style-book/names-and-titles/.

In terms of how *Mr* interacts with images to contribute to the representations of Muslims and Islam in the *Telegraph*, one interpretation could be that it helps to construct parity, where Muslims are nominated in a similar manner to non-Muslims. As the term *Mr* conveys respect, it makes articles appear to be less negatively biased towards the person who is being written about. However, this interpretation does not chime with our earlier analyses of the *Telegraph*, which suggested representations associating Islam with conflict, angry protest and anti-Semitism. Perhaps, then, *Mr* functions as a legitimation strategy, helping the newspaper avoid criticism of less positive representations around certain types of people.

Of the 66 occurrences of the Times' top keyword, *writes*, 51 occur in a pattern involving an opening bracket followed by a person's full name, then the word *writes*, then a closing bracket (e.g. 'Martyn Ziegler writes'). These cases refer to journalists and can sometimes involve articles where numerous journalists have worked on different parts of the story. These articles therefore involve somewhat dramatic stories which can take multiple perspectives. For example, an article entitled 'Biden pledges to replenish Israel's Iron Dome missile system – as it happened' (10 October 2023) reports on the following: a statement from President Joe Biden about Hamas; criticisms by British home secretary, Suella Braverman; comments by the president of the World Bank; a meeting between Joe Biden and Bejamin Netanyahu; a report on bodies of Israelis killed by Hamas; opinion from the IMF on the impact of the conflict; and President Erdogan of Turkey's offer of intervention in the conflict. Each of these sections has a different author preceded by the word 'writes', indicating who contributed towards the various parts.

The most distinctive images associated with *writes* tend to be either of politicians (Podium and FlagOfTheUnitedStates, the latter which usually appears with pictures of Joe Biden), crime and policing (HighVisibilityClothing and Security) or war and bombings (Atmosphere, Pollution, Car, Night, LandVehicle and Horizon).

These *Times* articles therefore show a more in-depth and wide-reaching analysis of news stories than articles from other newspapers, linking together a range of different international responses to global events. In terms of how this links specifically to representation of Islam and Muslims, though, the focus tends to be on associating them with war and conflict.

6.6 Stage 6: Comparison of Methods

In this final stage we provide answers to research question 1, regarding the extent to which the image tags provide new insights into the analysis of news discourse.

First, all of the stages of analysis we performed were valuable in shedding light on the distinctive representations of Islam and Muslims across the nine newspapers. In some cases, the analyses of the text and images directed us to focus on different kinds of representations. For instance, the *Guardian* keywords tended to relate to criticisms of the government's counter-terrorism program while the *Guardian* key image tags directed us to articles about King Charles and his views on Islam. In considering just the text we identified the sometimes complex motivations behind some of the articles. Examination of the keywords made it clear which newspapers tended to have more negative representations of Muslims and Islam (the *Daily Mail*, *Daily Star*, *Express*, *Sun*, *Telegraph* and *Times*) and which ones were more positive (the *Guardian*, *Independent* and *Mirror*). However, the keywords also revealed other agendas. The *Daily Mail* and *Express* also wanted to represent the Labour Party negatively, so wrote about its leader coming into conflict with Muslims. The *Mirror*'s positive representations of Ramadan were supplemented with advertorials for chocolate advent calendars, and the *Times* was able to combine criticism of the SNP with criticism of Islam through negative articles about its leader, Humza Yousaf. A wider finding of our analysis is that there is often a dual agenda occurring in articles about Islam, where the aim is not just to represent Islam but to achieve some other purpose (e.g. criticising a political party or encouraging readers to purchase a product).

In other cases, the different analytical approaches confirmed representations we had already seen or helped to strengthen them. The multimodal analysis showed how images often acted in concert with the text to produce a more emotive effect. For example, the analysis of an *Independent* keyword, *hate*, indicated that it was often used in stories about hate crimes directed at Muslims. The fact that these stories also included photographs of a six-year-old boy who had been murdered in a hate crime and of his grieving father at a press conference helped to personalise the stories, giving them a stronger impact. Similarly, stories aimed at painting Keir Starmer in a negative light in the *Express* were helped by image choices which showed him at less than his best, caught in mid-speech or with poor lighting. Sometimes, then, the images provided a clearer view of a newspaper's stance on a topic.

At other times, the images helped us to identify a representation which was not found through analysis of the text. The *Daily Mail*'s use of images that were tagged as Crowd indicated a form of representation that was based on collectivisation of Muslims, showing them all performing the same act (e.g. praying or protesting) in a way which removed individuality. Other *Daily Mail* images, which showed angry acts of protest or injured children, helped to legitimate the newspaper's negative stance towards Hamas.

The ways that people were dressed in images were also relevant. For example, pictures tagged as Tie and DressShirt tended to depict (usually male) politicians, helping to emphasise their powerful stance. This was sometimes contrasted with images of 'ordinary people', as in the *Daily Mail* articles which showed Muslim council members in the US who had banned displays of pride flags. Also, consider the stories in the Daily Star which quoted women who challenged Islam's gender norms. Such stories were often accompanied by sexualised images of these women in swimwear or underwear, suggesting that the articles were not only intended to be seen as being about challenges to Islam. Facial expressions such as smiles were one way that people could be characterised positively, and we also note the high number of images tagged with Smile from *Mirror* articles about Ramadan, or the *Express* photos of Keir Starmer, which tended not to show him smiling.

Even the more abstract image tags led to insights. The tags Line, Pattern and Rectangle attributed to *Guardian* images were related to positive representations of King Charles III through the issue of new stamps which included Islam, while the colour red was used in images in the *Times* and *Telegraph* as a way of symbolising the Labour Party. Sometimes the investigation of text surrounding an image tag revealed an aspect of a story that couldn't have been predicted, allowing us to make links to representations in other parts of the corpus. For example, analysis of the *Daily Mail* keyword *council* revealed that it related to stories from the US about Muslims gaining positions of power and making controversial decisions. Meanwhile, analysis of text related to the image tag Room in the *Independent* revealed stories which showed American Muslims as victims of hate crimes. Both newspapers use the US as a source of stories, reporting on the cases which contribute towards the desired representation. Due to the shared language and cultural influences of the US and UK, stories from the US take on a somewhat prophetic resonance, with the implication that 'it could happen here' (the UK), although the two newspapers focus on very different aspects of US life as it relates to Islam.

Our analysis was limited in that in stages 1 and 2 (Sections 6.1 and 6.2) we only considered the top 10 keywords and top 10 key image tags for each newspaper, while stages 4 and 5 (Sections 6.4 and 6.5) involved a more in-depth analysis of a single key image tag or a single keyword for each newspaper. Focussing on just the top keywords or key image tags enables us to avoid accusations that we cherry-picked items that would perhaps have produced the most interesting findings. And while there was enough variation among these top items to allow us to cover numerous aspects of the corpus, it also meant that some items produced fewer insights than others. In particular, the keywords *Mr* and *writes* in the *Telegraph* and *Times*, respectively, were more indicative of stylistic aspects of these two newspapers. This indicates that in a future study where we might not be as concerned with evaluating methods, we would probably want to be more selective about which features of the corpus we devoted time to.

Yet overall, including the images in the analysis gave us a more accurate sense of what the articles were aiming to achieve and how they went about it. Although some articles used images for informational purposes (particularly those which showed maps or graphs), which aided clarity, other images appeared to aim for an emotional (or, in the case of the *Star* and *Sun*, a sexual) response from readers. Reading about a six-year-old boy who has been stabbed in a hate crime is likely to provoke a strong reaction, but seeing a picture of the boy at his birthday party makes the story unforgettable. We end this final stage, then, by arguing that there was definitely value in including the images in the analysis.

7 Conclusion

In this concluding section we reflect on our findings and some of the implications of them, providing a more critical perspective of what we were able to achieve, as well as considering directions for future research.

To answer research question 2, in our analysis of distinctive representations of Islam across the nine newspapers we found a mixed picture, with representations broadly being linked to each newspaper's political position: the more conservative the newspaper, the less positive the representation. There were also differences between tabloids and broadsheets, with the former tending to deal in more extreme forms of representation, showing sexualised and violent images more than the latter. Baker et al. (2013) noted that one of the defining aspects of UK press coverage of Islam was to frame it around conflict, and this was a finding which, to some extent, applies to the present corpus, with the Israel–Hamas conflict providing material for stories on bombings, global protests and political disagreements.

However, we also noticed differences between the Baker et al. (2013) study and the present one. Negative stories around Muslim women wearing veils, Muslims receiving government assistance or Muslims as easily offended did not appear as salient in this corpus, and although we did find a few stories about Muslims with extremist views, they were fewer in number than in the earlier corpus. Instead, we found that some newspapers had informational stories which related to Islamic practices like Ramadan and the Hajj, and while there were articles which collectivised Muslims and also presented them as similar to one another (especially through images of Muslims praying or protesting), there were also some which emphasised diversity among Muslims. Other articles represented Muslims as victims of hate crime, and there was more acceptance of the existence of Islamophobia. Even the conservative newspapers appeared to have toned down their more egregious uses of language compared to what was found in Baker et al. (2013), and while negative representations still existed, they were more implicit, relying, for example, on choosing to quote people who were critical or reporting stories from the US about Muslims gaining power in local councils. Some conservative practices, however, appear to be resistant to change. In Baker et al. (2013), we noted how the *Daily Mail* used the spelling 'Moslem', despite being asked by the Muslim Council of Britain to adopt the spelling 'Muslim', as the former spelling is similar to the Arabic word for oppressor. In our more recent corpus, the *Daily Mail* now used 'Muslim', but it spelled 'Qur'an' as 'Koran', in spite of the fact that 'Koran' is not the preferred spelling. However, our overall picture is that there are a wider range of representations of Islam and Muslims in our 2023 corpus, with the negative ones being more subtle.

There are a number of possible reasons for these changes. The most notable of these is increasing awareness and criticism around newspaper discourse in the UK in recent years, emerging out of academic research but also linked to organisations like the Centre for Media Monitoring, which produces detailed reports on news representations of Islam, while lobbying journalists and editors. Additionally, pressure groups like Stop Funding Hate have engaged in social media campaigns which encourage people to lobby advertisers to remove support from publications that foster hate and division. And, in the last decade, newspapers have had to increasingly compete with a much wider range of other news sources, including television channels and online news. A study by Statista (2024) found that the most popular news source in the UK was the television channel BBC One (used by 43% of people in 2024). This was followed by ITV, Facebook, BBC iPlayer, Sky News, BBC News Channel, the BBC website or app, Instagram, Twitter, Channel, 4, WhatsApp and Google. Only then do we see one of the newspapers in our corpus appearing: the *Daily Mail* (accessed by 13% of people, and down from 18% in 2019). Although it could be argued that newspapers still have political influence (and their talking points can influence other news sources), they are no longer the dominant monoliths that they used to be.

While Jones and Unsworth (2022) found that Muslims were the second least favoured group in the UK (disliked by 25.9% of the public), there is also evidence that attitudes in the UK towards Islam are gradually becoming more positive. A survey by More in Common (2024) found that the majority (54%) of people aged 18–24 had positive views towards Muslims, with this figure being

42% for the 25–40 age group, 31% for 41–54, 28% for 55–74 and 26% for over 75s. If younger people retain these views, attitudes will gradually become more positive over the years. The dialectical nature of news discourse means that it must both influence and reflect popular discourses. Or, put more simply, while newspapers have some power to shift opinion, people will stop reading newspapers or openly criticise them if they publish views they disagree with.

Moving on to the methodological aspects of this Element, we now want to critically consider how we carried out our analysis and what lessons for the future we could take away. First, we evaluated tagging accuracy and removed tags which were frequently inaccurate, but we did not devote time to considering whether the tags themselves were actually useful to the analysis. The corpus contained 1,743 unique tags, resembling a Zipfian curve (Figure 2), with few frequent tags and many tags that only occurred a small number of times. (Over half of the tags occurred fewer than five times.) This suggests that images used in the corpus tended to have many similarities with one another, with frequent tags indicating a prevalence of crowd scenes and the outdoors, as well as portrait pictures of people. It is perhaps reassuring that Smile was the fourth most frequent tag in the corpus, although we did not find tags like Sad, Scowl, Frown or NeutralExpression so it isn't possible to ascertain if people are shown smiling more often than looking unhappy. Comparing different sections of a corpus or different corpora together would help to establish whether Smile is relatively more frequent in a particular corpus, but the idiosyncrasies of the tagging system can make other forms of comparison difficult. The lack of tags relating to identity characteristics meant that some of the most obvious comparisons that could have been made were not, although certain tags like Tie, LongHair and Beard acted as approximate indicators of (typically performed) gender. The tagger does allow users to train the model using their own data which have been annotated with custom-created tags, so potentially tags like Frown could be added if needed, and a useful direction for future research could involve analysis where the standard annotation system has been supplemented with tags which were deemed to be of interest. Another issue with the tagger involves the specificity of tags. For example, there were numerous tags relating to vehicles (e.g. Bicycle, BicycleFrame, BicycleHandlebar, BicycleSaddle and BicyclePart), with some images receiving several of these tags. This suggests that frequencies of tags relating to vehicles are likely to be somewhat inflated in the corpus. Such tags might be useful if, say, bicycles were important to the analysis, but for our purposes just having one tag (Bicycle) would probably be sufficient. Every occurrence of a tag in the corpus will impact calculations of keyness and collocation, so decisions around which tags to retain or remove have wider consequences. This is something that could also be considered more carefully in future projects: not just which tags are accurate, but which tags are duplicating information unnecessarily.

The corpus tool we created, Image Tag Explorer, vastly improved the way the analysis was conducted by Baker and Collins (2023), enabling us to view images associated with particular newspapers, tags or words. However, it did not enable concordance views, so images did not appear within their immediate textual context, requiring manual work in order to root out image and full-text combinations. Typically, a concordance table is useful in terms of presenting multiple citations of the same word so users can spot linguistic patterns by looking up and down the list. A problem with supplementing a concordance table like this with images is that each image would be rather small if they had to fit at the end of a concordance line, so perhaps we need to rethink what a concordance looks like if it involves images. One option could be to present images in a grid, with the relevant textual context underneath each item. In order to help identify linguistic patterns, frequently recurring words or phrases could be emboldened or coloured. Another option could be to have slightly larger concordance lines, which would allow images to be presented at the end of each line as thumbnails, which would be enlarged if the user hovered the mouse over them.

One challenge in writing this Element relates to reproducing images from the newspapers. While written text under 400 words long can generally be quoted in academic papers, as long as it is used as part of criticism or analysis, permissions must be obtained (and often purchased) when reproducing images that have been analysed. For many of the images in our corpus it was not possible to obtain permissions, so they could only be described, rather than shown, as part of the analysis. Newspapers regularly obtain images from commercial sites like Getty and Alamy, and it was possible to identify their origins and purchase licences to reprint some pictures. However, such images are not cheap to obtain and sometimes have to be purchased by the author (a picture can literally cost more than a thousand words). Some publishers allow images to be converted to line drawings so they can be displayed without seeking copyright clearance, but not all do this. These issues of access and cost place an impediment to multimodal corpus research and may influence the kinds of projects that people engage in.

Similarly, the task of building the multimodal corpus was more complex than it is in projects which only collect written text. Despite the fact that we were able to use Python scripts to automate the process, which made the data collection viable in the first place, this still entailed a significant amount of work, since a different text extraction approach had to be developed for each of the nine newspapers due to the different web layouts used. Projects like this currently require knowledge of coding which is likely beyond the experience of many corpus linguists, requiring teams with different skills to work together (and perhaps also requiring access to funding in order to employ computer scientists to build the corpora or develop tools to analyse them). As well as the software to analyse multimodal corpora, it is also hoped that tools can be developed in order to more easily automate the process of building and tagging such corpora.

A further outcome of this Element was the blueprint it provides for how manual evaluations of AI image tagging can be carried out systematically. It is essential to emphasise the importance of using manual evaluations as checkpoints to ensure that the automated tags broadly align with human interpretation and contextual understanding. While AI models can process vast amounts of data with impressive speed and at a much lower cost when compared to manual image analyses, AI image tagging is still prone to errors and biases that can skew analysis, and the tagging process is not transparent. Manual evaluations are therefore paramount to identifying these discrepancies and ensuring the robustness and credibility of multimodal corpus approaches.

We should not overstate what current image taggers are capable of. Currently, Vertex AI cannot provide a complete account of all the visual elements of an image, nor can it show how they relate to one another to create meaning or provide the kinds of interpretative analyses that only a human researcher can carry out. The tool is able to direct researchers to salient or frequent aspects of images across a corpus that may have been missed, as well as identify how such aspects co-occur with linguistic elements in texts. Future generations of tools may be able to go beyond this, although it is cautioned that such tools should be aids to human analysis and insight, rather than replace them.

In summary, this Element demonstrates the transformative potential of multimodal corpus linguistics in enhancing our understanding of complex discourse patterns and we hope that it inspires further research in this area. The effort invested in constructing a news corpus with image tags yielded profound insights, particularly in terms of nuanced representations of Islam and Muslims. This innovative approach proved invaluable, despite the extra effort that went into building the news corpus, since the inclusion of image tags brought a new dimension to the analysis. The approach allowed the analysts to understand the patterns of news discourse around Islam and Muslims much more clearly than if they had just considered the written text. There are numerous areas of research where this kind of approach could be taken in future. Apart from news discourse, social media is one obvious area where multimodal corpus analysis would be fruitful. Other interesting sources could involve children's fiction, educational textbooks, adverts, political pamphlets or health information. Our study indicates that a potentially exciting new form of corpus analysis is now available, offering a truly multimodal perspective and deeper insights into the texts we engage with.

References

Awass, O. (1996). The representation of Islam in the American media. *Hamdard Islamicus*, 19(3): 87–102.

Baker, P. (2023a). Associations between Islam, extremism, and terrorism in the British national press 1998–2019. In S. Al-Azami (ed.), *Media Language on Islam and Muslims*. Cham: Palgrave Macmillan, pp. 83–106.

Baker, P. (2023b). *Using Corpora for Discourse Analysis*. Second edition. London: Bloomsbury.

Baker, P. and Collins, L. (2023). Creating and analysing a multimodal corpus of news texts with Google Cloud Vision's automatic image tagger. *Applied Corpus Linguistics*, 3(1).

Baker, P., Gabrielatos, C. and McEnery. T. (2013). *Discourse Analysis and Media Attitudes: The Representation of Islam in the British Press*. Cambridge: Cambridge University Press.

Bednarek M. and Caple H. (2012). 'Value added': Language, image and news values. *Discourse, Context & Media*, 1(2–3): 103–113.

Bednarek, M. and Caple, H. (2014). Why do news values matter? Towards a new methodological *Tijdschrit voor Economische en Sociale Geografie* framework for analysing news discourse in critical discourse analysis and beyond. *Discourse & Society*, 25(2): 135–158.

Bednarek, M. and Caple, H. (2017). *The Discourse of News Values*. Oxford: Oxford University Press.

Brookes, G. and Curry, N (2024). The changing discourses on Islamophobia in the UK press: A modern-diachronic corpus-assisted study. *Journal of Corpora and Discourse Studies*, 7: 101–124.

Christiansen, A., Dance, W. and Wild, A. (2020). Constructing corpora from images and text: An introduction to visual constituent analysis. In S. Rüdiger and D. Dayter (eds.) *Corpus Approaches to Social Media*. Amsterdam: John Benjamins, pp. 149–174.

Collins, L. C. (2020). Working with images and emoji in the Dukki Facebook Corpus. In S. Rüdiger and D. Dayter (eds.) *Corpus Approaches to Social Media*. Amsterdam: John Benjamins, pp. 175–196.

Dunn, K. (2001). Representations of Islam in the politics of mosque development in Sydney. *Tijdschrit voor Economische en Sociale Geografie*, 92(3): 291–308.

Gabrielatos, C. (2018). Keyness analysis: Nature, metrics and techniques. In C. Taylor and A. Marchi (eds.) *Corpus Approaches to Discourse: A Critical Review*. Oxford: Routledge, pp. 225–258.

Galtung J. and Rüge M. H. (1965). The structure of foreign news. *Journal of Peace Research*, 2(1): 64–91.

Garside, R. (1996). The robust tagging of unrestricted text: The BNC experience. In J. Thomas and M. Short (eds.) *Using Corpora for Language Research: Studies in the Honour of Geoffrey Leech*. London: Longman, pp. 167–180.

Gatt, A., Tanti, M., Muscat, A., Paggio, P., Farrugia, R. A., Borg, C., Camilleri, K. P., Rosner, M. and van der Plas L. (2018). Face2Text: Collecting an annotated image description corpus for the generation of rich face descriptions. Proceedings of the 11th Edition of the Languages and Evaluation Conference (LREC 18), 3323–3328. https://aclanthology.org/L18-1.pdf.

Heuer, C. A., McClure, K. J. and Puhl, R. M. (2011). Obesity stigma in online news: A visual content analysis. *Journal of Health Communication*, 16(9), 976–987.

Jones, R. and Unsworth, L. (2022). *The Dinner Table Prejudice: Islamophobia in Contemporary Britain*. University of Birmingham. Retrieved from www.birmingham.ac.uk/documents/college-artslaw/ptr/90172-univ73islamophobia-in-the-uk-report-final.pdf.

Kress, G. and van Leeuwen, T. (20202020). *Reading Images: The Grammar of Visual Design*. Third edition. London: Routledge.

McClure, K. J., Puhl, R. M. and Heuer, C. A. (2011). Obesity in the news: Do photographic images of obese persons influence antifat attitudes? *Journal of Health Communication*, 16(4): 359–371.

McGlashan, M. (2016). The representation of same-sex parents in children's picturebooks: A corpus-assisted multi-modal critical discourse analysis. Unpublished PhD thesis, Lancaster University, Lancaster.

McGlashan, M. (2021). Linguistic and visual trends in the representation of two-mum and two-dad couples in children's picturebooks. In A. J. Moya-Guijarro and E. Ventola (eds.) *A Multimodal Approach to Challenging Gender Stereotypes in Children's Picture Books*. London: Routledge, pp. 213–238.

Mey, G. and Dietrich, M. (2017). From text to image: Shaping a visual grounded theory methodology. *Historical Social Research / Historische Sozialforschung*, 42(4): 280–300.

Moore, K., Mason, P., and Lewis, J. (2008). *Images of Islam in the UK: The Representation of British Muslims in the National Print News Media 2000–2008* (monograph). Cardiff School of Journalism, Media and Cultural Studies. http://jppsg.ac.uk/jomec/resources/08channel4-dispatches.pdf.

More in Common (2024). *How prevalent is anti-Muslim prejudice in the UK?* 3 March 2024. www.moreincommon.org.uk/blog/how-prevalent-is-anti-mus lim-prejudice-in-the-uk/.

Nikolajeva, M. and Scott, C. (2000). The dynamics of picturebook communication. *Children's Literature in Education*, 31(4): 225–239.

O'Donnell, M. (2008). Demonstration of the UAM CorpusTool for text and image annotation. Proceedings of the ACL-08: HLT Demo Session (Companion Volume), 13–16. Association for Computational Linguistics. https://aclanthology.org/P08-4004.

Pearce, M. (2001). 'Getting behind the image': Personality politics in a Labour Party election broadcast. *Language and Literature*, 10(3), 211–228.

Peez, G. (2006). Fotoanalyse nach Verfahrensregeln der Objektiven Hermeneutik. In W. Marotzki and H. Niesyto (eds.) *Bildinterpretation und Bildverstehen. Methodische Ansätze aus sozialwissenschaftlicher, kunst- und medienpädagogischer Perspektive.* Wiesbaden: VS Verlag für Sozialwissenschaften, pp. 121–41.

Poole, E. (2002). *Reporting Islam: Media Presentations of British Muslims.* London: I. B. Tauris.

Rafiee, A., Spooren, W. and Sanders, J. (2021). Framing similar issues differently: A cross-cultural discourse analysis of news images. *Social Semiotics*, 33(3): 515–538.

Richardson, J. E. (2004). *(Mis)Representing Islam: The Racism and Rhetoric of British Broadsheet Newspapers.* Amsterdam: John Benjamins.

Scott, M. (1997). PC analysis of key words – and key key words. *System*, 25(2): 233–245.

Scott, M. (2024). *WordSmith Tools Version 9* (64 bit version). Stroud: Lexical Analysis Software.

Scott, M. and Tribble, C. (2006). *Textual Patterns: Key Words and Corpus Analysis in Language Education.* Amsterdam: John Benjamins.

Sibai, D. and Jaworska, S. (2024). Triangulating visual and textual corpus-assisted discourse analysis to study social actor representations: The case of Saudi women in the British and Saudi news media. *Corpora*, 19(1): 61–92.

Smith, N., McEnery, T. and Ivanic, R. (1998). Issues in transcribing a corpus of children's handwritten projects. *Literary and Linguistic Computing*, 13(4): 217–225.

Statista (2024). Leading news sources in the United Kingdom (UK) from 2018 to 2024. www.statista.com/statistics/266709/leading-news-sources-in-the-uk/.

UN-OCHA. (2024). Reported impact snapshot | Gaza Strip (16 October 2024). United Nations Office for the Coordination of Humanitarian Affairs. www .ochaopt.org/content/reported-impact-snapshot-gaza-strip-16-october-2024.

Van Leeuwen, T. (2008). *Discourse and Practice: New Tools for Critical Discourse Analysis*. Oxford: Oxford University Press.

Wilson, A. and Thomas, J. A. (1997). Semantic annotation. In R. Garside, G. Leech and A. McEnery (eds.) *Corpus Annotation: Linguistic Information from Computer Text Corpora*. London: Longman, pp. 53–65.

Acknowledgements

This research was made possible by Research England funding and supported by the Centre for Media Monitoring, London.

Printed by Integrated Books International,
United States of America